The Art of Deception

For Ben,

Love and Congratulations

Billy

graduation '75

The Art of
Deception

Nicholas Capaldi

PROMETHEUS BOOKS

an ethical humanist press

923 Kensington Ave.
Buffalo, New York 14215

SBN 87869-004-2

Library of Congress Catalog Card Number 79-154983

Printed in the United States of America

© 1971 by DONALD W. BROWN INC.
60 East 55th Street
New York, N.Y. 10022

Acknowledgements

I wish to thank Mrs. Amy Pryor for her assistance with this book. I also wish to acknowledge a special debt to my colleague James Jordan for his many helpful suggestions in improving the text.

Contents

Preface

This book is about what has traditionally been called informal logic. Informal logic is as old as logic itself, having been treated by the first and greatest of all logicians, Aristotle. Its description as "informal" is in contrast with "formal" logic which includes the treatment of the syllogism and, in modern times, the treatment of symbolic or mathematical logic. At the same time, informal connotes something which is undisciplined if not disorganized. This brings us to the main point: the currently disorganized state of informal logic.

There are few serious and lengthy treatments of the subject. More often than not, a chapter or two on informal logic is all that one finds in the standard logic textbooks and treatises; most histories of logic disregard the subject altogether. Moreover, the actual treatments of informal logic found in different sources reveal almost no uniformity. The only common assumption made by those who analyze informal logic is the implicit one that all informal logic is illogical or a collection of errors. There is no recognition of, and hence no attempt to explain, the underlying distinctions between the correct and incorrect use of this logic. If logic can be abused, then quite obviously it can also be used.

What is even more bewildering is the informal if not sloppy way in which the errors of informal logic are analyzed. No two lists of such errors are the same. Even the Latin names traditionally used to identify and codify these errors are not used uniformly. It is analogous to a situation in which every library had its own way of classifying books and where in some cases the same subject headings were used by different libraries but had different meanings. The upshot is that most treatments of informal logic result in lists of so-called fallacies resembling the listings in a telephone book. To make matters worse, the authors or collectors of these lists vie with each other to enumerate the greatest number of fallacies. One author comes up with a list of thirty-four, but he is quickly superseded by another author who has discovered over one hundred fallacies! There is even a certain amount of creativity and ingenuity that goes into these lists, for one finds authors who simply invent a name and add the word fallacy to describe any piece of reasoning with which they disagree.

One day I expect to find people who collect fallacies forming a society much as those who collect stamps. In addition they will anxiously await the publication of the next catalogue in much the same way as thousands of people awaited the list of seventy-seven sins carefully enumerated by fundamentalist preachers. No doubt these people all are motivated by the desire to see if they are missing anything.

If I have correctly described the current state of informal logic, then I think teachers and students of logic can understand why the teaching of informal logic is usually so unsuccessful. Surely most of it is irrelevant by any standards. Surely we cannot expect anyone to master a "telephone book." If we do, then we should not be surprised that even after a course in informal logic most students are as incapable of spotting a fallacy as they were before they took the course, a point which various studies have verified. Another key factor in this failure to teach students to deal with fallacies in real life is the emphasis upon recognition. Typically, the student or reader is asked to identify fallacies in the writings of others, and, although he must respond, his response is within a primarily passive situation. This narrow textbook approach necessitates that the author or teacher rely upon singularly obvious or simple-minded examples. The transfer to other contexts is rarely made.

In order to circumvent this difficulty and to give the reader an active grasp of informal logic, I have adopted a different technique in my approach. In addition to presenting an organized approach to the subject, I have written this book from the point of view of one who wishes to deceive or mislead others. On the assumption that "it takes one to know one," I have found that people are able to detect the misuse or abuse of logic if they are themselves the masters of the art of deception. I ask the reader to contemplate the prospect of a world in which everyone knew, really knew, how to use and thereby detect the misuse of logic.

To exemplify this perspective, I wish to use an analogy with writings on politics. There are at least three great books which seek to describe political reality: Aristotle's *Politics*, Hobbes's *Leviathan*, and Machiavelli's *The Prince*. Aristotle fails because he is so dull that he is often not read, while Hobbes's perceptiveness is lost in the controversy over the theoretical context in which he embeds his insights. Machiavelli's vivid account is the most popular and the most effective. I believe that more readers have learned about politics from reading Machiavelli than anyone else precisely because Machiavelli's *Prince* is presented in a format of active manipulation rather than passive recognition. I hope that my presentation of informal logic will have the same kind of impact as Machiavelli.

The Art of Deception

CHAPTER ONE

Presenting Your Case

In presenting your case to other people, there are several general considerations which must be kept in mind. First, you must have a clear idea of just what your case, issue, or point of view is. Second, you must be aware of the relation of your position on this case or issue to your position on other issues. The reason for this is obvious. You do not want to present your case on one issue in such a way that it might cause conflicts or future embarrassments when you present your position on another issue. Third, you should have some clear idea of the audience to whom you are presenting your case. Are they people who already share your opinion, are they undecided, or are they likely to be unreceptive or openly hostile? No doubt your audience may consist of any combination of the foregoing possibilities. Different audiences will require different approaches. Fourth, you must understand the medium you are using to convey your case. Are you speaking directly to the people, or are you writing an article for a newspaper, magazine, scholarly journal? Are you preparing an advertisement which will be visually presented for a few moments; an audio commercial which lasts thirty seconds; a mimeographed sheet which will be read in one minute and discarded; a placard to be waved about, etc., etc? Finally, you must constantly keep in the forefront of your mind the purpose for which you are presenting your case. If you are a rational teacher trying to present an objective case you will do one thing (like considering the shortcomings of your position), and if you are trying to get people to buy a product you will do something else (like pretending that there are no weaknesses in your product).

The last point is worth dwelling upon. If you know what you want to achieve (your purpose), and if you know the people with whom you want to achieve your end (your audience), and the means available to you (medium), then you will be better able to achieve your end. No doubt there are all kinds of clever and brilliant things you might do, but it is equally clear that some of these clever and brilliant things may be irrelevant, in which case they may detract attention from your main purpose or even be counterproductive. If you remember that the important thing is winning, then you are not likely to go off in all directions at once. Analogously, there is no reason for leading a dazzling and disastrous cavalry charge (however immortal this may make you in the hearts of poets) when a simple artillery barrage will do the job.

In the discussion to follow, I will assume that the audience is either present, in which case the presentation is oral, or that the audience is being communicated with through some journalistic medium. Where more specialized audiences are involved, I shall note the special techniques required. Otherwise it is to be assumed that the audience is listening to your speech or reading it.

The presentation of your case should be given in

three main parts: arousing sympathy for your cause; presenting facts or what will be taken as facts to substantiate your case; and driving home the conclusion. The first three parts of this chapter will consider each of these in greater detail. The fourth will consider some nonverbal techniques to be used in presenting your case.

Gaining a Sympathetic Audience

The notion that one can engage in argumentation by simply launching into the presentation of information is a foolish one. No discussion, and certainly no argument, can exist in a vacuum. Everyone, including the speaker and the audience, has a frame of reference in terms of which he speaks and to which he implicitly or explicitly appeals. It is essential that you keep this frame of reference in mind when presenting your case. If you want to prepare the audience for the presentation of your point of view and to gain a sympathetic hearing as well, then appeal to the common frame of reference which you share with the audience.

Appeal to Pity.

To appeal to pity is to appeal to the emotions of your audience, emotions which you expect to be favorably directed to your cause. The most effective use of the appeal to pity does *not* involve the use of highly emotive and inflammatory language; rather it relies upon the bare presentation of simple and unchallengeable facts. It is important that this appeal not be overdone so that members of the audience are not unnecessarily antagonized. This is especially true when the audience is not well known to you or when they are still undecided about the issue raised.

Appeals to pity are found most frequently in courts of law where attorneys attempt to gain a sympathetic hearing for their clients. An example is to be found in the case of a young man who is on trial for burning down the house of his parents while they were sleeping and who has thus been charged with homicide. His attorney pleads for mercy on the grounds that the young man is now an orphan!

The most famous, and in a way clever and ironic, use of the appeal to pity is the one directed by Socrates to the jury trying him on the charges of impiety and corrupting the youth of Athens. The famous trial is described in Plato's dialogue entitled *Apology*. (Jowett translation amended by N. Capaldi)

Perhaps there may be some one who is offended at me, when he calls to mind how he himself, on a similar or even a less serious occasion, prayed and entreated the judges with many tears, and how he produced his children in court, which was a moving spectacle, together with a host of relations and friends; whereas I, who am probably in danger of my life, will do none of these things. The contrast may occur to his mind, and he may be set against me, and vote in anger because he is displeased at me on this account. Now if there be such a person among you—mind, I do not say that there is—to him I may fairly reply: My friend, I am a man, and like other men, a creature of flesh and blood, and not "Of wood or stone," as Homer says; and I have a family, yes, and sons, O Athenians, three in number, one almost a man, and two others who are still young; and yet I will not bring any of them hither in order to petition you for an acquittal. And why not? Not from any self-assertion or want of respect for you. . . . But, having regard to public opinion, I feel that such conduct would be discreditable to myself, and to you, and to the whole state. . . . And I say that these things ought not to be done by those of us who have a reputation; and if they are done, you ought not to permit them; you ought rather to show that you are far more disposed to condemn the man who gets up a doleful scene and makes the city ridiculous, than him who holds his peace.

Another well known example of the appeal to pity is to be found in Marc Antony's speech in Shakespeare's play *Julius Caesar* (Act III, Scene 2):

> Friends, Romans, countrymen, lend me your ears;
> I come to bury Caesar, not to praise him.
> The evil that men do lives after them;
> The good is oft interred with their bones;
> So let it be with Caesar. The noble Brutus
> Hath told you Caesar was ambitious;
> If it were so, it was a grievous fault,
> And grievously hath Caesar answered it.
> Here, under leave of Brutus and the rest,—
> For Brutus is an honourable man;
> So are they all, all honourable men,—
> Come I to speak in Caesar's funeral.
> He was my friend, faithful and just to me:
> But Brutus says he was ambitious;
> And Brutus is an honourable man.
> He hath brought many captives to Rome,
> Whose ransoms did the general coffers fill:
> Did this in Caesar seem ambitious?
> When that the poor have cried, Caesar hath wept;
> Ambition should be made of sterner stuff:
> Yet Brutus says he was ambitious;
> And Brutus is an honourable man.
> You all did see that on the Lupercal
> I thrice presented him a kingly crown,
> Which he did thrice refuse: was this ambition?
> Yet Brutus says he was ambitious;
> And, sure, he is an honourable man.
> I speak not to disprove what Brutus spoke,

But here I am to speak what I do know.
You all did love him once, not without cause:
What cause withholds you then to mourn for him?
O judgment, thou art fled to brutish beasts,
And men have lost their reason. Bear with me;
My heart is in the coffin there with Caesar,
And I must pause till it come back to me.

In a more contemporary vein, there are many examples of the presentation of an argument which begins
with an appeal to pity. In presenting a case against the
use of drugs or in favoring the imposition of a policy to
curb drug addiction, we might begin by describing the
life and death of a twelve-year-old boy who became a
heroin addict. In arguing for pacificism, we might describe the horrors of war as in a description of the after-
math of the dropping of an atomic bomb on Hiroshima.
The critics of the Vietnam War have effectively employed the reading of lists of war dead as an appeal to
pity. On the other hand, those who favor the policy of a
strong military posture and preparedness might present
their case by beginning with a description of the bombing of Pearl Harbor or a description of the concentration
campus at Auschwitz, pointing out how these were
partly the result of political isolationism.

Appeal to Authority.

To appeal to authority is to inform your audience
that prominent people are in favor of the position which
you are urging. The appeal to authority, like the appeal
to pity, is an attempt to establish a frame of reference
for the rest of your case. There is nothing inherently
wrong with this appeal; rather it is essential to any discussion. No one can know everything nor can he be
everywhere at once. We are all forced to take for

granted that other people are sometimes experts in their fields and that they are reliable sources of information. If the people who are engaged in a discussion, argument, or dispute cannot agree on authorities, then the prospects of a successful resolution are very dim indeed. Moreover, if you can appeal to the right authorities, you are also guaranteeing a more sympathetic hearing for your case.

There are at least eight qualifications which should be kept in mind when citing authorities. First, you should be sure that the authority you cite is not considered a liar by members of your audience. A man convicted of perjury is hardly a credible witness. A political leader who has once misled people loses his credibility in the eyes of the public. Adlai Stevenson suffered this fate in the United Nations because he at one critical moment denied that the United States had supported the invasion of Cuba during the Bay of Pigs episode.

Second, you must present authorities who are considered disinterested by the audience, that is, authorities who do not have a vested interest in the case you are discussing. The reason for this should be obvious. A man with a vested interest is tempted, either consciously or unconsciously, to construe things in his own favor. Naturally, this makes him an unreliable authority. In certain technical fields it is next to impossible to misconstrue the facts. Thus, in the case of handwriting analysis, ballistics, or chemical analysis, it is difficult to conceive of an interested authority. Anyway, it is always possible to find a disinterested one if you are sure that the facts will be on your side.

On the other hand, there are certain fields where finding a disinterested authority is next to impossible.

I am thinking in particular about politics. Putting aside for the moment the question of whether there is even such a thing as an authority on political matters, there is the ever present problem of separating a disinterested analysis of a political situation from the interests, wants, needs, or hopes of the person doing the analysis. In an area such as this the closest thing to an authority would be someone with a distinguished record of predictions, even where those predictions ran contrary to the *known* interests of the predictor.

Examples of people whose possible interests might disqualify them as authorities worthy of being invoked follow. A stock broker whose profits come from the volume of securities sold is not to be considered a disinterested authority on what to expect from the stock market. Such an interest can only be offset if the broker can substantiate the fact that he has successfully predicted in the past and that he has advised people against investing at certain times. In such a way he is establishing his integrity. In discussing appropriations for the military budget, it must be kept in mind that prominent military men have a vested interest in getting the largest appropriation possible. At the same time, members of the academic and research communities who have traditionally argued against large or increased military expenditures stand to gain themselves from a smaller military expenditure since there would be more funds available for the expansion of college and research facilities. Hence, they too might have a vested interest in such a controversy.

Third, the authority should be considered conscientious by the audience about the area in which he claims expertise. A man who is not careful about details will soon cease to be considered an authority. Moreover, an expert who relies upon the assistance of a large staff must be sure about the diligence of his staff. A cabinet officer who relies upon a huge bureaucracy can easily be tempted into accepting a report and then presenting it to the public without careful scrutiny. Most of us have noticed how painstakingly some scientists will make claims or to what lengths they will go in qualifying the implications of their research. Usually, it is the headline hunting journalist who makes excessive claims.

Fourth, when an authority is invoked it is best to make sure that the authority is well known. Quoting authorities who are not known to be authorities in their fields, at least not known by your audience, is ineffective. For example, when discussing child rearing, it might be more impressive to refer to Gesell or Spock than to Dr. John Smith. "Well known" in this case is always to be determined by reference to your specific audience. Although a man is generally well known, he may not be well known in a particular area or to a particular audience. Conversely, when addressing a specific audience it might be better to quote the local expert than the internationally famous one.

Fifth, the authority used must be an expert in the relevant field. Dr. Spock may be a well-known expert in the field of child care, but can one say honestly that he is an expert in international relations in particular and politics in general? When discussing physics, it would seem natural to use physicists as authorities; when discussing the possibilities of using the sea to grow food, the relevant authorities would be marine biologists, etc. To invoke an authority in one field as an expert in another, perhaps totally unrelated, field opens one to all kinds of damaging attacks. For example, a man once claimed to have invented a truly effective cigarette filter and offered to promote it under the sponsorship of Columbia University of New York City. Columbia may have an outstanding reputation in general as a university, but this in no way implies that everything associated with it is outstanding. Combined with a lack of conscientiousness on the part of some Columbia administrators, this carelessness led to all sorts of embarrassments. As far as I know, that filter is still unavailable.

The one important exception to the foregoing qualification of invoking authorities concerns the use of celebrities, prominent members of society either theatrical or "aristocratic." In a sense, these people are not necessarily experts in anything. However, their sheer prominence will attract attention to a cause or position in a way that no other appeal can match. On the assumption that one can provide relevant experts, there is no objection to supplementing those experts with celebrities who are not experts. A case in point concerns the campaign of the American Cancer Society to discourage cigarette smoking. There is no question that the American Cancer Society can provide authoritative evidence from medical authorities who are beyond reproach. But in addition to this authority, the society has employed well-known actors to dramatize the connection between cigarette smoking and cancer. This campaign has been highly effective.

Thus we see how qualification four (well known) and qualification five (relevant expert) may supplement each other. At the same time, we should not forget qualification three (being conscientious). One of the actors employed for the cigarette-danger campaign of the American Cancer Society was later arrested in London for the possession of marijuana.

Sixth, if possible, the authorities cited should be

both current and historical. The more technical the issue, the more current should be your authority. Thus, in medical matters, possibly a question about the heart, Dr. Christian Barnard is more to be respected as an authority than Galen or Hippocrates. Statistical studies especially should be as fresh as possible. On the other hand, if one can find historical authority to supplement current authority, this has a way of making one's case even stronger. George Washington has a way of popping up in all kinds of arguments. He is sometimes paired with Senator Fulbright (the former as historical and the latter as current authority) as an expert in arguing against entangling foreign alliances. I have also seen Washington invoked as a proponent, at least implicitly, of marijuana since he allegedly grew hemp in his fields and it was widely used during the eighteenth century to treat bronchitis. Here Washington might be paired with Timothy Leary, a current proponent of drug use.

Seventh, the authority cited should have an opinion which is representative of the general expertise in his field. The word "representative" is a tricky one to define, but it can perhaps be made clear through some examples. A great physicist may share many opinions with his colleagues, but he may also have some highly idiosyncratic opinions, especially in controversial areas which are not shared or even are opposed by his colleagues. A nuclear physicist who literally believes that life exists on other planets holds an unrepresentative opinion. In 1936, when Franklin D. Roosevelt was running for president of the United States, over two-thirds of the newspapers in the country were editorially opposed to his re-election. This percentage in no way represented the actual feeling of the community or even the people who actually worked for these newspapers.

It was an opinion which simply reflected the position of those who owned the newspapers.

The eighth qualification is that the authorities should be as numerous, as diverse, and otherwise as different as possible. If you can find two authorities with otherwise conflicting opinions who nevertheless agree with your position on a specific issue, this tends to impress the audience with the fact that you are so right that almost everyone has to agree with you. For example, it would be foolish to quote the editorial opinion of one newspaper twice in order to support your case. Obviously once is enough. On the other hand, if you live in an area with two or more newspapers which usually have conflicting editorial frames of reference, but they for once agree on your position, then it is very impressive to quote from both. Newspapers may support different political candidates, but they are all likely to support a campaign to do away with pollution.

Appeal to Tradition. (Sacred Cows)

The appeal to tradition, also known as the *ad populum* appeal, is the appeal to an ideal, a theoretical or abstract principle to which all people—or at the very least the members of your audience—pay lip service. No doubt some people take these ideals more seriously than do other people, but everyone claims to respect them. This is an important principle of argumentation because it is one of those principles that establishes the frame of reference of the discussion. If you cannot find this common point then there cannot be any discussion at all. (You should keep in mind that this is definitely not an appeal to precedent, which will be discussed in the next subsection.)

An example of the appeal to tradition is Martin

Luther King's invoking the principle of nonviolence. While there are certainly those who would not under similar circumstances use nonviolence or even those who do not subscribe to the principle in their heart of hearts, it is still the case that few would openly attack someone else's advocacy of nonviolence. The appeal to nonviolence is an appeal to a tradition which has deep moral, political, social, and religious roots, roots which spread beyond any one culture or historical period. To invoke nonviolence is to gain a tremendous sympathetic reaction on the part of audiences. We might also add that this principle can frequently disarm enemies as well.

Appeal to Precedent.

To appeal to precedent is to appeal to cases or instances similar to the one being defended. It is not necessary that everyone agree with your precedent, as in the case of the appeal to tradition. Precedents must be real or actual as opposed to traditions which are ideal. In fact, we frequently appeal to precedent when we cannot find a tradition to help us, but it must be recognized that this kind of appeal is a calculated risk in that it automatically antagonizes some part of the audience.

Violent revolution is a precedent in American life as is obvious from our Revolutionary War and the Civil War, but it would be odd indeed to say that violent revolution is one of our ideals. When H. Rap Brown allegedly said that "violence is as American as apple pie," he was appealing to precedent and not to tradition.

The appeal to precedent is found most frequently in law courts where attorneys must search for cases previously decided in order to buttress their present case. If the courts, especially higher courts, have made decisions favorable to one "kind" of issue and if an attorney believes that his present case belongs to that "kind" or category, then he appeals to that decision or series of decisions as precedents. Needless to add, the other attorneys must find different precedents or show how the case does not fit the alleged "kind."

There is a story about a fig newton told by an ex-Supreme Court Justice. Imagine one company suing another company, where both companies produce pastry and baked goods. The suit concerns patent rights. Company A claims that it owns a patent for a specific kind of cookie and that Company B has violated the patent by making a similar cookie. Company B claims that its product is different because it is not a cookie but a fig newton. When is a change a change? If the judge favors Company A he decides that the patent right has been violated, whereas if he supports Company B he might say that the product is really a fig newton and does not fall under the cookie patent. There are endless precedents, and finding the right one for your case involves (a) ingenuity in your research, and (b) knowing what appeals to your audience. Judges are not the only ones with definite tastes.

Presenting the Facts

Statistics.

The purpose of this section is to show how the facts or the accepted truth should be used in presenting your case. The minor theme can be summed up in the statement that half a truth is sometimes better than no truth at all.

ceived 36 percent of the vote; and Marchi, who received 22 percent of the vote. How would you analyze these statistics? Those who favored the candidacy of Lindsay stressed the facts that he (a) won, (b) had more votes than either of his rivals, and (c) clearly defeated his nearest rival. In fact, this way exactly how *The New York Times* reported the election results. Given their frame of reference, what they said was true. On the other hand, the opposition could clearly point out that Lindsay had not won a majority of the vote but a plurality and that, in fact, almost 60 percent of the voters of New York City had rejected him. Given their frame of reference, what these people said was also true.

One of the things that Procaccino could have argued for was an election law reform which implemented run-offs until one candidate clearly had a majority of the vote. However, he could not really invoke this principle since he himself had won the Democratic Party nomination in the same way that Lindsay ultimately won the final election.

In our second example, let us imagine that a large and important corporation that deals in retail sales has just reported its financial record for the year. The relevant, and true, figures are as follows:

Earnings: (a) 1 percent of sales, *or*
(b) one percent on a dollar, *or*
(c) 12 percent on investment, *or*
(d) $5,000,000 profit, *or*
(e) 40 percent increase in profits over 1939, *or*
(f) 60 percent decrease in profits over last year.

All of these figures say exactly the same thing. A retail organization takes in a large gross but actual net

In an age such as ours, the most convincing kind of evidence is statistical evidence. What boy does not know the batting average, to three decimal places, of his favorite baseball player? How often have we heard one automobile praised at the expense of another because the former possesses a measurably greater horsepower or higher compression ratio? The underlying assumption in so much of our use of numbers seems to be that a higher number automatically indicates something better. The true mania for statistics knows no bounds, as witnessed by the body count employed by the Pentagon in the war in Vietnam. You cannot argue with numbers, except with other numbers.

Some general rules about using statistics follow. On the assumption that it is possible, always do the following when appealing to statistical evidence. First, make sure that the statistics come from a reliable source. Here all of the things we said about using authority will be relevant. The right source of statistical information can be epitomized in the expression "independent laboratory." Second, since statistical data are rarely uniform, they may be grouped or "interpreted" in different ways. Do not hesitate to use only that part of the statistical data which suits your case, especially if you do not expect to be challenged. For example, a national survey on how people feel about abortion may indicate that most or the majority are opposed to it. When the statistics are broken down by states, it may be that in your state the majority of the people favor it. Thus, if you wish to get a law passed favorable to abortions then quote the state statistics. If you wish to get a law passed against abortions then quote the national survey. In both cases you will be telling the truth.

This brings us to the third general rule, a rule we

In an age such as ours, the most convincing kind of evidence is statistical evidence. What boy does not know the batting average, to three decimal places, of his favorite baseball player? How often have we heard one automobile praised at the expense of another because the former possesses a measurably greater horsepower or higher compression ratio? The underlying assumption in so much of our use of numbers seems to be that a higher number automatically indicates something better. The true mania for statistics knows no bounds, as witnessed by the body count employed by the Pentagon in the war in Vietnam. You cannot argue with numbers, except with other numbers.

Some general rules about using statistics follow. On the assumption that it is possible, always do the following when appealing to statistical evidence. First, make sure that the statistics come from a reliable source. Here all of the things we said about using authority will be relevant. The right source of statistical information can be epitomized in the expression "independent laboratory." Second, since statistical data are rarely uniform, they may be grouped or "interpreted" in different ways. Do not hesitate to use only that part of the statistical data which suits your case, especially if you do not expect to be challenged. For example, a national survey on how people feel about abortion may indicate that most or the majority are opposed to it. When the statistics are broken down by states, it may be that in your state the majority of the people favor it. Thus, if you wish to get a law passed favorable to abortions then quote the state statistics. If you wish to get a law passed against abortions then quote the national survey. In both cases you will be telling the truth.

This brings us to the third general rule, a rule we

might dub "getting on the bandwagon." If you can show that most people, or the majority, support your position or opinion, then not only invoke that information as support or evidence that you are right, but also invite people or the audience, at least implicitly, to join the majority. No one likes to be left out in the cold.

An important variation of this general rule concerns the phrase "more people." How often have you heard the expression, "More people use Brand X than any other brand." What exactly does this mean? It can mean that 51 percent of all people use Brand X. It can also mean that only 12 percent of all people use Brand X. How is this possible? Suppose we have a situation in which there are sixteen competing brands of beer (or sixteen candidates for office). Isn't it possible that no one brand (or candidate) from among the sixteen has a majority and that the brand (or candidate) with the largest following has only 12 percent? It is not only possible but it would be true to say that Brand X (or candidate X) has more followers than any other brand (or candidate). The phrase "more people . . ." may be invoked and used just as if it meant a majority.

A fourth general rule concerns the use of large numbers. Invariably, large numbers impress people much more than small numbers. When you add to this the fact that even in our society most people do not really comprehend the use of statistics, percentages, and fractions, it is usually more effective to quote the large number rather than the percentage. It sounds better to say that candidate Smith received six million votes than to say he received 52 percent of the votes. Almost half of the people voted against Smith but he sounds more formidable when you say that six million people are behind him.

We should also add that where large numbers are involved repeating them tends to have a mathematically cumulative effect. It is said that when the Soviet Union grants foreign aid to a country it grants at least three times more aid than it actually gives. How is this possible? For example, first it is announced in the press that the Soviet Union *will* grant one million dollars worth of aid. Second, when aid is actually granted it is once more announced that the Soviet Union *is* granting one million dollars worth of aid. Finally, after the aid has been granted it is announced that the Soviet Union *has* granted one million dollars in aid. Many people would have the impression that three million dollars in aid was involved. Analogously, the same effect has been achieved by President Nixon when reporting on Vietnam troop withdrawals.

Fifth, just as large numbers tend to impress, so small numbers tend to be overlooked. This means that you may openly discount a small number or minimize its importance. An example of this was supplied by Yugoslavia's Marshal Tito. In discussing political parties, Tito once observed that America has two political parties while Yugoslavia has one. It is an insignificant difference because it is only a difference of one!

It is now time to turn to some actual cases of the use of statistical data. No number is important in itself. It is only with respect to some other number or to some frame of reference that a particular number acquires its significance. Hence the important thing is not simply collecting data but selecting the frame of reference within which you plan to use the data. Let us take as our first example the New York City mayoralty election of 1969. There were three candidates: Lindsay, who received 42 percent of the vote; Procaccino, who received 36 percent of the vote; and Marchi, who received 22 percent of the vote. How would you analyze these statistics? Those who favored the candidacy of Lindsay stressed the facts that he *(a)* won, *(b)* had more votes than either of his rivals, and *(c)* clearly defeated his nearest rival. In fact, this way exactly how *The New York Times* reported the election results. Given their frame of reference, what they said was true. On the other hand, the opposition could clearly point out that Lindsay had not won a majority of the vote but a plurality and that, in fact, almost 60 percent of the voters of New York City had rejected him. Given their frame of reference, what these people said was also true.

One of the things that Procaccino could have argued for was an election law reform which implemented run-offs until one candidate clearly had a majority of the vote. However, he could not really invoke this principle since he himself had won the Democratic Party nomination in the same way that Lindsay ultimately won the final election.

In our second example, let us imagine that a large and important corporation that deals in retail sales has just reported its financial record for the year. The relevant, and true, figures are as follows:

Earnings: (a) 1 percent of sales, *or*
           (b) one percent on a dollar, *or*
           (c) 12 percent on investment, *or*
           (d) $5,000,000 profit, *or*
           (e) 40 percent increase in profits over 1939, *or*
           (f) 60 percent decrease in profits over last year.

All of these figures say exactly the same thing. A retail organization takes in a large gross but actual net receipts after expenses are very small. The first two figures, (a) and (b) reflect this fact. You may begin to wonder how in the world any corporation stays in business or would want to stay in a business for such a small profit margin. The answer is that daily sales bring in a large amount of cash which can then be invested at high interest rates for the remainder of the year. We are all familiar with the fact that the larger the amount of money you can invest, the larger the percentage of the return. The same one percent may, by the end of the year, return twelve percent. By the end of the year, the actual profit in dollars may be, as in (d), $5,000,000. How does this profit compare with past performance? It all depends, again, on the frame of reference. If we choose the 1939 level as base period, profits have increased substantially. If we choose last year's profits as the frame of reference, profits may have decreased even though the company is still earning a profit.

How would these statistics be used? The management would use them as follows: in refuting an argument for price controls, the management will refer to (a); in reporting to the stockholders, the management will refer to either (c), (d), or (e); in bargaining with the unions, the management will refer to (f). The union, of course, will insist upon (d) and (e) in demanding higher wages and benefits for the employees. Dissident stockholders may seize upon either (f) or challenge (c) as being too low and the result of poor investments, suggesting the need for a new board of directors.

Let us take another example. In the graph below, we have reported the average income broken down by educational categories. As we go from left to right, income increases, and as we go from top to bottom educational attainment increases.

	under $5000	$10,000	$15,000	over $25,000
H.S. dropout	▬▬			
H.S. graduate	▬▬▬▬			
B.A.	▬▬▬▬▬▬▬▬▬			
M.A.	▬▬▬▬▬▬▬▬▬▬▬▬▬			
Ph.D.	▬▬▬▬▬▬▬▬▬▬			

In an effort to encourage students to gain as much education as possible, it has been frequently pointed out that income increases with education. The longer you stay in school, the more you are likely to earn during your lifetime. However, such an argument can be used only if we do not take into account the average earnings of Ph.D.'s. If we drop out the last line, the Ph.D. line, the case will be more convincing. Conversely, if we retain only the last two lines, we would have a good case against continuing on for the Ph.D. degree.

Perhaps the most useful word in the statistical arsenal is the word *average*. The term "average" may mean one of three different things. First, it may mean the arithmetical *mean*, which is the total divided by the number of people or entities involved; second, it may mean the *median*, which is the halfway point between the number of people or entities involved; third, it may mean the *mode*, which is the point where you find more people or entities on the scale than at any other point.

Our example of differing uses of the term average is taken from the reading scores of a seventh grade class of students. A test is administered to determine the level at which the students are reading. To be on grade level is to be able to read what students at that grade are expected to read. For the seventh grade student in our example, to be on grade level is to be able to read what the seventh grade student is expected to read. To be reading below grade level is to be unable to read what the seventh grade student is expected to read. To be reading above grade level is to be able to read not only what the seventh grade student is expected to read but also much more difficult pieces.

Grade Level	Number of Students
12	4
11	4
10	3
9	2
8	1
7	1 (arithmetical mean)
6	0
5	1 (median, 15 above, 15 below)
4	2
3	12 (mode)

If we use average to mean arithmetical mean, then the teacher can legitimately claim that the class is reading at its grade level. If we use average in the sense of either median or mode, then critics of the teacher can legitimately say that the average member of the class is not reading on grade level. It is obvious, of course, that a serious problem exists in this class and it is equally obvious that any attempt to understand the problem in terms of averages would be misleading.

Suppose that I am contemplating a change of residence, and that I am looking for a more equable climate. I begin by reading advertisements and I find two areas with annual mean temperatures of 75 degrees. That sounds fine. However, one of these areas has a temperature range from 65 degrees to 85 degrees, whereas the other area has a temperature range from 35 degrees to 115 degrees. Obviously, they are not equally desirable.

The important principle that we have seen at work time and time again is that the same information may be presented in different ways. The trick is to choose the way most useful to your case. *Question:* Should one use total numbers or percentages? *Answer:* It all depends. Suppose you wish to expose corruption in the police department or some other government agency, an exposure which you believe is useful in undermining public confidence in the present administration. Suppose that last year there was one conviction for bribery. Suppose that this year there have been two convictions for bribery. Instead of using total numbers, you should in this case use percentages. There has been a 100 percent increase in convictions for bribery, and heaven only knows about the unconvicted. On the other hand, if you are advertising a cold remedy which cures 2 percent of the people who use it and the major competing remedy cures 1.5 percent then you should use the total number involved and claim that your remedy cures more people than any other remedy.

It is difficult to follow statistical reports, especially if they are long, involved, and require that the members of your audience perform mental comparisons. In order to aid the presentation of your case, it is useful to represent your statistics in the form of a graph. There is no point in using graphs if they will not help your case, so here are some rules for maximizing the presentation -of evidence by graphs.

First, in order to exaggerate either the increase or decrease you wish to call to the attention of the audience, you may do one of two things: either present a graph with a missing legend, or blow up one part of the graph. Please keep in mind that at no time are we using false figures. This is purely an exercise in emphasis.

As an example, let us imagine someone trying to call attention to the increase in crime in specific areas. A true graph of the situation looks like this:

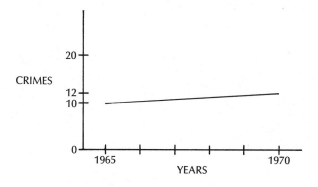

In order to highlight that increase you might remove a legend and present the graph as follows:

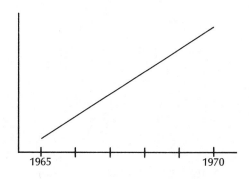

An even better graph is a blow-up to highlight the increase:

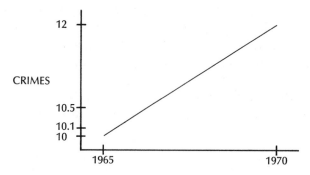

In addition to line graphs, you may also use bar charts. A special way for easing the mental anguish of your audience is to emphasize your point with cutouts. Below, we dramatically present the increase in the education budget:

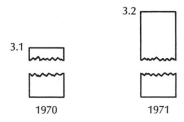

Another technique for dramatic effect is to confine measurement to one dimension and to manipulate the other dimensions. For example, an employer wishes to emphasize the increase in benefits he has extended to his employees. He shows a picture of two workers each sitting upon a pile of coins representing employee benefits before and after his conferring of benefits. The truth of the matter is that he has doubled the benefits and therefore the pile on the right is twice as high as the pile on the left. Yet, because the piles are also drawn to scale, the pile on the right is twice as wide as the pile on the left. In terms of volume, the pile on the right is four times as large even though benefits have only doubled.

BEFORE   AFTER

A final technique which should be kept in mind for dramatizing the presentation of statistical data is the translation of the data from one medium into another. Perhaps the most common instance of this is the equation of people with geography. There is, of course, no uniform relation between the size of an area in square miles and the population density of that area. Many large geographical areas have extremely small populations whereas small geographical areas have extremely high populations. If the support for your case is not impressive in one dimension or medium, then seek to express it in a more impressive medium. In presidential campaigns, for example, it is customary for the news media to show a map of the United States wherein each state has its electoral college vote figure and is shaded, or not, in order to show that it belongs to one candidate or another. This technique can be misleading or impressive, depending upon your point of view, because a candidate with a large electoral vote may have a small geographical presentation, whereas a candidate with a large geographical backing may have a small electoral vote. The positions are further detracted from or enhanced depending upon the number of bordering states a candidate has. The more connected in space his support is the more solid it appears; the more diffuse, the less solid. The only way to overcome this imbalance if you are victimized by it is to draw the map not to geographical scale, but in proportion to electoral vote. In the latter case, Rhode Island will be bigger than Alaska. The other compensatory maneuver is to collect supporting states together not by actual borders, but by position in support, or group them alphabetically.

Theoretical Constructs.

There are of course many ways to classify beliefs, but for our purposes it is enough to divide beliefs into two large groups: (a) raw data and (b) theory or theoretical constructs. Examples of raw data include such things as the names of people, the color of an automobile, the date, etc. Raw data may be briefly characterized as any information which has, is, or might be checked by observation. Theoretical constructs, on the other hand, are not things one can check by simple observation. They are the product of intellectual activity and are freely used to help integrate raw data. In the previous section on statistics we discussed statistics as raw data; in this section we shall discuss theoretical constructs and their use.

Let us sharpen the distinction by seeing how theoretical constructs are most effectively used, as in the domain of physical science. Scientists distinguish between observational terms such as color, weight, pressure, etc. (which refer to observable entities), and theoretical terms such as electron, psi function, etc. (which do not refer to things we see). Theoretical constructs are used to explain the raw data we observe. Boyle's law, for example, refers to observable terms: at a constant "temperature," the "volume" of a given quantity of any gas is inversely proportional to the "pressure" of the gas. On the other hand, the theory of ideal gases, which states that an ideal gas would consist of perfectly elastic molecules and that the volume occupied by the actual molecules and the forces of attraction between the molecules is zero or negligible, does not refer to anything observable but is used to explain why there is such a thing as Boyle's law. We infer that gases behave this way because we assume that a gas consist of perfectly elastic molecules.

Other examples of theoretical constructs abound. When Freudian psychoanalysts speak about the "Oedipus complex" they are not speaking about anything we observe but are employing a theoretical construct to explain raw data. When Marxists talk about economic "imperialism," the latter expression is not something which one sees but a construct to explain what is actually seen, e.g., colonies. When historians talk about the "French Revolution" they are not referring to a single event such as the storming of the Bastille, but rather invoking a theoretical construct to explain a whole series of events. When student radicals talk about the "Establishment," we realize that they are not referring to a specific person or event but offering a theory to explain a whole spectrum of events and activities.

The interesting thing about theoretical constructs is that they refer to nothing observable yet we use them to explain what we do observe. Since they refer to nothing observable they cannot literally be shown to be false. For example, if someone uses an observational term like "red," as in "your car is red," we check the

truth of his statement by looking at your car. If your
car is not red but blue, then his statement is false. On
the other hand, there is no way of conclusively checking
a theoretical construct, even in science. Although this
matter is too complicated for us to go into here, we may
note that if we found a gas which did not obey Boyle's
law our initial reaction would be to assume that there
is some obstruction or other cause or variable we have
not taken into account. To have constructs which cannot be disproven in one's arsenal is to possess a deadly
weapon.

Let us exemplify a theoretical construct in action.
Suppose I wish to argue the case that our society is
corrupt. I may invoke the theoretical construct that our
society is run by a secret clique or is the victim of a
superconspiracy. Suppose I am asked to produce evidence of this conspiracy. My reply is that all of my
evidence has been destroyed by the people behind the
conspiracy.

Another example, this time using some supporting
evidence, is an argument to the effect that Lincoln
never existed. Lincoln was a mythical figure invented
by a group of Northern industrialists who wanted to
seize control of the country. *Evidence:* The log-cabin
stories are too cornball to be believed. Nobody could
have written all of the beautiful speeches attributed to
Lincoln; obviously they were the work of a team of
speech writers. A careful examination of the portraits
of Lincoln show a great series of changes over the
years; just notice how his beard varies from period to
period; this could only be because a number of different
actors were hired to "play" the part of Lincoln. Finally,
when John Wilkes Booth shot "Lincoln" he was really
shooting a rival actor who got the "part" instead of him;

you will notice that Booth was not caught alive but shot before he could reveal the true story behind the conspiracy. Does this sound plausible?

Let us look at a final example and then compare it to the previous ones. In a hospital for the mentally ill there is a man who claims to be dead. In an effort to bring him back to his sanity, a doctor deliberately cuts the man in order to show that the man bleeds. The doctor triumphantly turns to the patient and declares, "You must be alive, you're bleeding." The patient merely replies, "That just goes to show that dead men can sometimes bleed."

It is not likely that most audiences would accept the theory of the inmate of the insane asylum. On the other hand, conspiracies always appeal to people. The trick here is to find theoretical constructs already in use and widely accepted by your audience and to use them as if they were the same thing as raw data. Despite the fact that it has no standing among many in the scientific community, Freudian psychoanalysis has so infected the popular mind that most people, or a good many of them, literally believe in such things as the unconscious, repression, Oedipus complex, etc. Generations of college students implicitly have accepted Marxist theories of history, economics, politics even though they are not aware that the theoretical constructs they are accepting are Marxist in origin. In argumentation, it is always a question of what your audience will fall for.

Classification.

In addition to presenting raw data, we must classify or organize it. Theoretical constructs are just one way of organizing or classifying information. There are several others.

All and some:

Avoid using the quantifiers "all" and "some." Do not say, "All good union members respond to strike calls"; rather say, "Good union members respond to strike calls." Why? If you do not use the word "all" you can still act as if you used the word "all" rather than the word "some." You want to avoid using "some" in your own presentation because your case will then sound too weak. The word "all," even implicitly, is much stronger sounding. At the same time, by not actually using the word you leave open the alternative of saying that you only meant to say "some," especially if your opponents challenge your statement later.

Continuum:

There are some vague classificatory terms which are part of a spectrum or continuum rather than extremes of a clear-cut division. For example, we can make a clear cut distinction between animals with a backbone (vertebrates) and animals without backbones (invertebrates). But there is no clear-cut distinction between bald and not bald people. How many hairs must a man have on his head in order not to be called bald? In such cases, you are at liberty to draw the line where it suits your convenience or vanity. Obviously anyone who challenges your distinctions in such cases is a quibbler.

Golden mean:

It is part of our general store of wisdom that the mean between two extremes is the most desirable position. Hence one should always aim to describe his position as a mean, a golden mean, between two undesirable extremes. The task here is to identify what constitutes the extremes in the minds of the audience.

In politics we have the following golden means:

The *moderate* is the mean between liberals and conservatives.

The *liberal* is the mean between radicals and reactionaries.

The *conservative* is the mean between fascists and socialists.

The *communist* is the mean between anarchists and revisionists.

Even in mathematics we can find the golden mean. If there is a dispute between two parties, one of whom claims that the sum of two and two is four and another of whom claims that the sum of two and two is six, we may claim that the sum of two and two is five. Remember that people love compromises.

One final word of advice: there are an infinite number of ways in which you may classify. The only limit is your own imagination.

Definition.

There is a classic point in every argument where a great outcry goes up that the participants involved should define their terms. We may call this the classical pause, and it is an important one. No one will really understand your case, including yourself, if you do not know the precise sense in which you are using your terms. There are three different ways in which you should be aware of your definitions.

First, there is the case of *truth by definition*. If your terms are defined carefully enough, and if your other factual data are correct, then your case is foolproof. For example, suppose I define the term "Enlightenment" at the very beginning of my argument as a term to cover Western European writers of the eighteenth century who believed that the method of science would eventually solve all human problems. Suppose, further, that I specify exactly the geographical boundaries of Western Europe, the temporal dimension of the eighteenth century, the exact nature of the scientific method, and what I mean by a human problem. Given this definition, I examine the writings of Jean-Jacques Rousseau. I find that he fits every specification except the implicit or explicit trust in scientific methodology. Hence I may conclude that Rousseau is not an Enlightenment writer. No doubt there will be historians of ideas and others who will immediately attack my exclusion of Rousseau and they may even show how many have classified Rousseau as an Enlightenment writer. But all of this is irrelevant in the light of my definition. My position remains invincible to all such attacks. Of course one could ask what value my definition has, but although this is a legitimate question it is a totally separate question from the question of whether Rousseau is an Enlightenment writer in view of my definition.

Second, there is the matter of *equivocation*. A specific term is said to be equivocal when it has more than one meaning. For example, the term "discrimination" has a positive connotation in cases where it means being selective on the basis of certain standards. A man may be said to have discriminating taste in his choice of clothes. "Discrimination" has a negative connotation in cases where it means to deny something to someone on purely arbitrary grounds. A man is said to discriminate when he refuses to serve Blacks in his restaurant. When you use equivocal terms, and there is nothing inherently wrong or even avoidable in these cases, you should be aware of the fact that the term is equivocal, and the precise sense in which you intend the term to be taken.

It is sometimes advantageous to specify the exact sense in advance if there is no alternative term and if you wish to capitalize on the possible value of that particular equivocal term.

On the other hand, it is sometimes advantageous not to specify the exact sense in which you wish a term to be taken. Here your motives may be that the term has a positive connotation to everyone and you wish to capitalize on this, but at the same time you want to leave open some alternative ways of interpreting that term. Politics in general, and diplomacy in particular, require the rigid use of equivocation. Take for example the term "neutrality." The term has a positive connotation; everyone respects a neutral. But exactly what does it mean? Neutrality may mean official spoken policy as opposed to actual practice. Neutrality may mean strict nonintervention of both word and deed. Neutrality may even mean the refusal to help one side while permitting a state of affairs which by negligence helps the opposing side.

A third definitional consideration concerns the possibility of really *creative thinking* (euphemism). The advance of human knowledge requires that new concepts be invented by man. This is certainly true of the sciences as witnessed by the importance of Newton's invention of calculus as a means for explaining motion through time. Without the invention of calculus we could not have modern physics. There is certainly no reason to discourage creativity in other realms as well.

Following is a list of some of the most creative concepts I have come across recently. They are phrases which incorporate (a) a traditional term which has a highly positive connotation, and (b) a qualification to cover new cases.

1. "genuine facsimile"—since the word "facsimile" is present, no one can claim that deception is being practiced here; at the same time, all of the value of the term "genuine" is achieved; the phrase as a whole simply means a highly detailed imitation.

2. "permanent guest artist"—of course a guest artist is not a regular or fulltime member; of course if you are permanent you are a regular or fulltime member; in fact, this is a category of special praise for someone who is otherwise a regular and fulltime member but not bound to rules which apply to others.

3. "Department of Defense"—this is a substitute for the Department of War; has anyone ever heard of declaring defense? This is a euphemism for an otherwise necessary evil and signifies, allegedly, that the country only fights in self-defense.

4. "selective pacifism"—we all know that pacifists will not fight under any set of circumstances; but, by being selective, one leaves open the possibility of fighting when he pleases and retains all moral aura of a pacifist. Is there any way of distinguishing behaviorally, not by rhetoric, among a pacifist of the selective persuasion, a militarist, and the normal type of behavior?

5. "nonviolent force"—you may now do anything you wish to do, even employ force, but the force is accompanied by the rhetoric of appeals to nonviolence.

6. "symbolic speech"—any act of behavior, other than speaking, which is illegal or immoral, may claim the protection of the first amendment on the grounds that it is symbolic speech.

7. "selective censorship"—one who appeals to this is not in favor of censorship; there are just *some* books and *some* people who ought not to be allowed public exposure. Is there a difference between this and pure unadulterated censorship?

8. "script assimilation" (otherwise known as forgery).

9. "social subtraction" (otherwise known as murder).

In conclusion, I should like to relate this section on definition to the section wherein I discussed gaining the sympathy of the audience. If you are going to be really creative in your thinking, then I suggest that you incorporate concepts which at least sound like the concepts you know that your audience accepts. Preferably you should follow up the very concepts or ideas you appealed to in that section of presenting your case.

Analogy.

When we assert an analogy, we are claiming that two things which are similar in one or more respects will be similar in another or future respect. Two things are analogous when they are similar in one or more respects. The greater the similarity the stronger will be the analogy. However, similarity is not identity. Hence there is always some point at which the analogy will break down. This is not necessarily a handicap since it is only important that the similarity holds in the respects which are relevant to what you would like to prove.

There are two kinds of analogies, literal and figurative. In a *literal* analogy we are arguing that:

A has properties $p_1, p_2, \ldots p_n, \ldots$ and p_x;

B has properties $p_1, p_2, \ldots p_n, \ldots$;

therefore, B has the property p_x.

This kind of literal analogy has been very successfully used in scientific research in constructing theories. For example, the Bohr theory of the atom was originally constructed along the model of the solar system (the nucleus is analogous to the sun and electrons are analogous to rotating planets, etc.). This model was later given up but it did prove to be extremely useful for a long time. In trying to discover cures for dread diseases, research scientists try to use analogies to other cures. For example, maybe cancer, like other diseases, is caused by a virus. Maybe inoculation will be a means of prevention. A map, in a sense, is analogous to the geographical area of which it is a map, although the area possesses properties which the map does not (for example, the geographical area is three dimensional while the map is usually two dimensional).

There is a difference between saying that A and B have different properties and saying that A and B have incompatible properties. When the analogy between A and B breaks down it is not because they have different properties, but rather because they have incompatible properties. For example, maps and the area described by the maps have different properties (two dimensions as opposed to three dimensions). However, it is conceivable that we can have a three dimensional map. On the other hand, there is an incompatibility between methadone (heroin substitute) and a vitamin pill. Methadone is a heroin substitute or synthetic which is used to treat addicts. Despite all of its benefits, methadone is addictive whereas a vitamin pill is not, even though both are analogously preventing something. Here the analogy suffers a serious incompatibility and breakdown. In short, before using a literal analogy make sure that there is no incompatibility with the major point you are trying to prove.

Figurative (*illustrative*) analogies are not meant to show literal similarities and structures or functions. Rather, they are literary devices for dramatically exemplifying a point. If you use figurative analogies you should make sure that the analogy is definitely positive and favorable to your case. At the same time, the analogy should reinforce the kind of sympathy-appealing devices you used in the first part of your presentation. At all times the predisposition of the audience should be kept in mind.

An example of a figurative analogy which is at the same time an example of an *ad populum* appeal is the so-called "ship-of-state." You should also note in the following examples the extent to which a clever person can take the same metaphor of a ship of state and come out with a different conclusion.

1. Thomas Carlyle: "Running a government is like running a ship; we need a strong hand at the helm."

2. Henrik Ibsen: "Society is like a ship; everyone must be prepared to take the helm."

3. Alexis de Tocqueville: "Like the navigator he [the statesman] may direct the vessel which bears him along but he can neither change its structure nor raise the winds nor lull the waters which swell beneath him."

4. J. M. Beck: "The constitution is neither, on the one hand, a Gibraltar Rock, which wholly resists the ceaseless washing of time and circumstance, nor is it, on the other hand, a sandy beach which is slowly destroyed by the erosions of the waves. It is rather to be likened to a floating dock, which, while firmly attached to its moorings, and not therefore at the caprice of the waves, yet rises and falls with the tide of time and circumstances."

Another figurative analogy which is at the same time a way of reinforcing the appeal to pity is the analogy between crime and disease. In his book *Erewhon*, which is "nowhere" misspelled backwards, Samuel Butler both satirizes Victorian England and argues that any distinction between crime and disease is ridiculous. In

Erewhon anyone who commits a crime is "cured," whereas anyone who becomes ill, say a person who contracts tuberculosis, is punished.

This is what I gathered. That in that country if a man falls into ill health, or catches any disorder, or fails bodily in any way before he is seventy years old, he is tried before a jury of his countrymen, and if convicted is held up to public scorn and sentenced more or less severely as the case may be. There are subdivisions of illness into crimes and misdemeanors as with offenses amongst ourselves—a man being punished very heavily for serious illness, while failure of eyes or hearing in one over sixty-five, who has had good health hitherto, is dealt with by fine only, or imprisonment in default of payment. But if a man forges a cheque, or sets his house on fire, or robs with violence from the person, or does any other such things as are criminal in our own country, he is either taken to a hospital and most carefully tended at public expense, or if he is in good circumstances, he lets it be known to all his friends that he is suffering from a severe fit of immorality. . . . Bad conduct . . . is nevertheless held to be the result of either pre-natal or post-natal misfortune. . . . The judge said that he acknowledged the probable truth, namely, that the prisoner was born of unhealthy parents, or had been starved in infancy, or had met with some accidents which had developed consumption . . . he knew all of this, and regretted that the protection of society obliged him to inflict additional pain. . . . The judge was fully persuaded that the infliction of pain upon the weak and sickly was the only means of preventing weakness and sickness from spreading, and that ten times the suffering now inflicted upon the accused was eventually warded off from others by the present apparent severity. I could therefore perfectly understand his inflicting whatever pain he might consider necessary in order to prevent so bad an example from spreading further and lowering the Erewhinian standard; but it seemed almost childish to tell the prisoner that he could have been in good health, if he had been more fortunate in his constitution, and been exposed to less hardships when he was a boy.

An example of a provocative analogy which might conceivably serve as either a literal or a figurative analogy is the one between Marxism and Christianity. As far as I know, Bertrand Russell was the first to call attention to the parallels in his *History of Western Philosophy:*

To understand Marx psychologically, one should use the following dictionary:

Yahweh = Dialectical Materialism
The Messiah = Marx
The Elect = The Proletariat
The Church = The Communist Party
The Second Coming = The Revolution
Hell = Punishment of the Capitalists
The Millenium = The Communist Commonwealth

The terms on the left give the emotional content of the terms on the right, and it is this emotional content, familiar to those who have had a Chrisian or a Jewish upbringing, that makes Marx's eschatology credible. . . .

Lewis Feuer has used this same analogy and even extended it a bit: ". . . like other creeds, it has its sacred text, its saints, its heretics, its elect, its holy city. If Marx was its Messiah, Lenin was its Saint Paul."

Driving Home the Conclusion

The point you are trying to make, the case you are presenting, must be epitomized in the conclusion. Everything you have done up until now was just preparation for the conclusion. First, you have tried to gain the implicit trust of the audience; second, you have presented data for the express purpose of backing up your conclusion. Naturally you should have had your conclusion in mind when selecting the information to present. The question we raise now is how and in what form that conclusion should be presented.

There are certain key words and phrases which not only signify to the audience that you are drawing the conclusion but at the same time reinforce in the minds of the members of the audience that your conclusion is the right one. The following key words and phrases should be used profusely when stating the conclusion:

1. obviously
2. certainly
3. there is no question that . . .
4. of course
5. surely
6. it is clearly evident that . . .

Evidence and conclusion are related to each other in at least one of two ways. Either the conclusion is a specific instance and the evidence consists of generalizations under which the specific instance falls, *or* the conclusion is a generalization and the evidence consists of specific instances which support the conclusion.

Let us look at the first possibility:

generalization ⟶ specific.

In arguing for a conclusion about something specific—let's say the prohibition of marijuana—we may appeal to the generalization that all drugs are or should be prohibited unless given under medical supervision. Another example would be the justification of rebelling against the present administration or the government of the United States by appeal to the precedent (here serving as a generalization) of revolution in American life. Here one claims kinship with Patrick Henry and

John Hancock. Once your audience has accepted certain generalizations, generalizations which you presented in the first two parts of your presentation, they must accept the conclusion.

Let us now examine the second possibility:

specific ⟶ generalization.

Statistical evidence is more often than not an example of going from specific cases to a general conclusion. Political polls of voter opinion are now frequently used as justifications for making policy decisions for the whole country. In fact, one might argue that elections are simply crucial polls.

There are other examples. Suppose I form an all-star basketball team made up of individuals who are acknowledged to be the greatest players. I choose Wilt Chamberlain, Oscar Robertson, Jerry West, Billy Cunningham, and Willis Reed. From these specific stars I might conclude that the team as a whole will be a star team or a great team.

As a final example, let us imagine two opponents each trying to argue for the same general conclusion of how to prevent war, any war. One side argues that the arms race or the stockpiling of weapons has always preceded a major war. Hence if we do not have an arms race we shall not have a war. The other side argues that the lack of military preparedness on one side incites aggression in others. It even produces as evidence the same debate in England in the 1930s where much to their later chagrin many prominent people argued against a military-industrial complex. Hence preparedness is the only way to prevent war. Both sides are appealing to different specific examples.

It is, of course, possible to defend a position or a conclusion by using both general and specific information. In fact, the strongest arguments usually have this double-barreled kind of support. Suppose we want to defend the conclusion that prostitution ought to be legalized. We might appeal to the general principle of free enterprise which encourages everyone to compete in an open market and offer any product or service he can to the public. By not having legalized prostitution (with medical supervision) we are encouraging an illegal monopoly on the part of the Mafia or others. Moreover, and here we appeal to specific statistical evidence, 10 percent of the population has or has had venereal disease, and at the present rate more than half the country will have venereal disease in seven years.

In the initial presentation, only positive evidence should be presented on behalf of your case. Other kinds of support will be considered later when we discuss rebuttals. In addition to achieving one end, any means or course we pursue is bound to have other consequences. Any rational person considers *all* of the consequences before selecting a specific remedy. This truth is of great value in the presentation of an argument. In addition to presenting evidence for why your position or point of view is correct, there is no reason in the world why you should not point out the residual benefits of your solution. In fact, a long list of residual benefits frequently serves as the deciding factor.

To begin with, act as if your solution had only positive residual benefits. Second, know what problems outside of the one under discussion are most on the minds of the audience. Third, claim that each and every one of these major problems will also be solved or at the very least ameliorated by adopting your position on the specific issue discussed. Although this tactic may cause some shock and surprise, I maintain that the only limitation on this procedure is your imagination.

Let us consider some examples. Suppose I am arguing against the use of marijuana and in favor of strong laws prohibiting its distribution and use. I might add as a residual benefit that the generation gap is caused by or exacerbated by the use of marijuana. Adopt my solution and you solve both problems. Even the cold war can be defrosted if our youth are clear-headed, and they can only be clear-headed if they are not smoking pot. Now let me argue for the legalization of the use of marijuana. Legalize pot, and even encourage parents to smoke it rather than drinking alcoholic beverages, and you will bring the generations together. Moreover, if everyone sat around smoking pot and making love, no one would ever feel aggressive enough to want to make war.

The real clincher to any conclusion is the use of *emotive language,* either positively toward what you favor or negatively toward what you oppose. If you are absolutely sure that your audience is with you, then you can wrap up your presentation by simply restating your conclusion in emotive terminology.

Consider the following summation presented to a Southern jury by Matt Murphy in defense of a white man being tried for murder:

And this white woman who got killed? White woman? Where's that NAACP card? I thought I'd never see the day when Communists and niggers and white niggers and Jews were flying under the banner of the United Nations flag, not the American flag we fought for. . . . I'm proud to be a white man and I'm proud that I stand up on my feet for white supremacy. Not black supremacy; not the mixing and mongrelization of races . . . not the Zionists that run that bunch of niggers. The white people are not gonna run before them. And when white people join up to 'em they become white niggers. . . .

The substance of Mr. Murphy's plea is quite simple even if controversial. He and therefore his client are of a certain ideology and the slain woman was of an opposed ideology. Further, he believes that the audience shares his client's ideology and will therefore excuse the act which is never denied. Yet it is the way in which this content is conveyed rather than the content itself that is all important.

That different statements can convey, at least minimally, the same information but with different connotations or emotional impact is best exemplified in another Bertrand Russell quotation, the conjugation of firmness: "I am firm; you are obstinate; he is pig-headed."

Politics abounds in emotive terminology; in fact, sometimes it is impossible to enter a political discussion without falling entirely into this mode of speech. Take the example of Richard Nixon. The minimum of facts are clear: he lost the presidential election of 1960 and then lost the race for governor of California in 1962. After the second loss he announced his retirement from seeking further political office. Several years later he was campaigning again and finally won the presidency in 1968. How would you describe this state of affairs? Mr. Nixon changed his mind? Mr. Nixon reversed himself? Mr. Nixon was impelled by circumstances to reconsider his decision? Mr. Nixon is a liar? To follow any political discussion for comprehension we have to separate that discussion into two parts: information conveyed and the emotional reaction of approval or disapproval.

Newspaper headlines, not just the editorials, are also slanted emotionally and are frequently designed to be that way. I have in mind one event the facts of which I will not convey. Rather I simply repeat the headlines

from different newspapers and let the reader decide
what he thinks happened:

STATE TROOPERS GUN DOWN STUDENTS

TWO STUDENTS SHOT IN GUNFIRE EXCHANGE WITH POLICE

MURDER ON CAMPUS

COPS FORCED TO KILL IN SELF-DEFENSE

NONVERBAL DEVICES

The discussion of emotive terminology leads naturally to a discussion of the other subliminal devices of
which one must be aware in presenting an argument.
As Marshall McLuhan never tires of repeating, the
medium is the message. Here again, your assessment of
the audience is crucial. What preconceptions do they
have that you wish to use? Find out what these are and
the nonverbal devices are obvious.

For example, clothing is important. A boy was
arrested for the possession of marijuana. The boy had
typically long hair and hippie clothing when arrested.
By the time his trial hearing came up his entire appearance had changed: short haircut and Brooks Brothers
suit. Obviously someone had given him the word that
"hippie types" were discriminated against, but everyone
forgives a clean-cut youth.

In oral presentation, voice is important. Your voice
must be sincere and confident, but above all it must be
deep. Absolutely everyone I know is impressed by a
deep voice and there are even exercises you can perform
to deepen your voice. Facial expressions and eye movements are also important in this respect. The general
rule here is to look people straight in the eye and never
have shifty eyes. People with shifty eyes are automat-

ically considered devious whereas any man who looks you straight in the eye must be honest.

The nature of the room or general surroundings are also important. I have heard a story to the effect that FBI director Hoover stands on a raised platform behind his desk when meeting an agent for the first time. The principle implied seems to be that added height adds stature as well, and it is true that we are impressed by tall men.

Bismarck had a great reputation for diplomacy. He frequently victimized lesser men (lesser from a chemical point of view) by insisting upon serving champagne throughout negotiations. Part of his secret was his ability to consume large amounts of alcohol without losing control of himself or the situation.

The most accomplished use of surroundings I know of is in the work of Billy Graham. His public speaking places are decorated with flowers and flags, his audiences primed by singing and other means until they slowly reach a crescendo for his own talk.

Not to be forgotten in any discussion of nonverbal techniques is the use of technological innovations. The latest and most effective seems to be video tape. The great advantages of video tape are that it can be edited for maximum effect and you cannot cross-examine a tape. The latter is especially important if your tape has the currently fashionable quasidocumentary style. The only way you can counter this is with another tape edited to show your point of view.

Examples of the use of film abound. The French director Godard seems obsessed with using the medium solely for propaganda purposes. In the 1964 Democratic National Convention, a film was shown depicting the life and family ties of the assassinated President John F.

Kennedy. Even the opposition itself was reduced to tears.

ADVERTISING AS A CASE STUDY

In advertising we find many of the techniques discussed above developed into a fine art. Especially instructive is advertising's almost complete reliance upon *positive* argument. Let us follow the foregoing outline and see to what extent advertising exemplifies each of the foregoing principles.

To begin with the advertiser must identify his market, break it down into its meaningful components such as geography, age, sex, etc., and the objectives he hopes to achieve in his advertising. Second, he must identify his product with the dual hope of (1) explaining the product in terms of the consumers' wants and needs, and (2) emphasize the individuality or superiority of his product over rival products. It is important to note, however, that the latter must be done in a subtle manner.

Getting a sympathetic audience:

In the case of advertising this means creating a conscious or felt need for the product.

a) *appeal to pity:* This works in two ways in advertising: either directly for the product or service, or indirectly through pity for those who need the product. As an example of the first kind we may note the Avis car rental commercials and advertisements which call attention to the *fact* that Avis is only number 2 (Hertz is first) and as a result has to try harder. Here the appeal to pity is an appeal to the American sympathy for the underdog. As an example of the second kind we may note advertisements for exercise programs for ninety-pound weaklings and our sympathy for them is extended to any product attempting to help them cope with a cruel world.

b) *appeal to authority:* This has to be either the first or second most prominent device used in the world of advertising. Examples are incredibly numerous. One patent medicine designed to relieve headaches and various other assorted ills notes that it contains more of the ingredient most recommended by doctors. Whatever that ingredient is, the mere fact that it is recommended by someone in a position of authority, namely the doctor or doctors, makes this an appeal to authority. Several toothpastes have a "kind" of endorsement from the American Dental Association. For those who are too cynical about medical authority or for those who are not sophisticated enough to care, there is always the vitamin-enriched bread endorsed by the famous athlete.

c) *appeal to tradition:* There are several interesting variations on this theme. First, we all know the name of Napoleon's favorite brandy, and if the Napoleonic legend is something that appeals to you, then so will this brandy—which happens to be good in spite of Napoleon. Closer to home is Dolly Madison ice cream. Now I do not know the exact connection between Dolly Madison (wife of President James Madison) and the present product. It is true that Dolly Madison was the first to make ice cream in America. But what exactly does this imply? Is ice cream as American as apple pie? Must one use Dolly Madison ice cream on pie à la mode?

The latest and most impressive use of an appeal to tradition, the attempt to show that one's product is consistent with a generally accepted ideal, is at the same time a factual appeal. Some detergents are now chemically produced so that they do not pollute our waters. This is not only an appeal to a traditional value but a very subtle way of noting the superiority of one product over another. Without some form of advertising most of us would never know this fact.

As a final example I note that some products have a union label attached to them so that anyone who is favorably disposed to unions may choose that product over its rivals.

d) *appeal to precedent:* The advertising counterpart to an appeal to precedent is the testimonial. Of course the testimonial is also an appeal to authority. If I can present letters of gratitude or interviews expressing enthusiasm for a product by people who sincerely claim that the product fulfilled their needs, then I have established precedents for your thinking that the product will help you. Here it is important that the precedents be like the potential purchaser. A celebrity is an appeal to authority. That means that famous people are out in a strict appeal to precedent and that the common man or the "housewife" are to be favored. For example, Oleg Cassini no doubt sends his shirts to a top commercial laundry, or maybe he does not have to wear the same one twice. On the other hand, John Doe, who can only afford to own two dress shirts, has a wife who is interested in a bleach that will get the yellow stains out of his shirt collars. Hence Mrs. Doe is more interested in a precedent (testimonial) from Mrs. Smith or Jones, etc.

Presenting the facts:
In advertising this means providing support for the contention that your product satisfies the need you have aroused in the previous part of your presentation.

a) *statistics:* What mother has not waited for her

son to run home and say, "Look Mom, no cavities," or, "Look Mom, 40 percent fewer cavities." There are several toothpastes which can present documentary evidence of statistical surveys which show that their product is superior in preventing tooth decay. Again, we have seen the bandwagon approach used often in advertising. If more people use Product A than any of its rivals, then clearly you should be using it too. We are also very familiar with the use of graphs. We know that Listerine kills more germs faster because we have actually seen the graph in action on television.

b) *theoretical constructs:* Advertisers are experts at seeing the world in a slightly different theoretical framework. This leads them to spot new entities and name them before the rest of us do. For example, one product claims to be a cure for "tired blood," which as far as I know is not part of the routine medical lexicon. Another product is supposed to be a remedy for "house-itosis," and if you do not know what that is you had better watch the commercial soon to find out whether or not your house or apartment suffers from it.

There is an important variation of the theme of theoretical constructs which we can call *accentuating the positive.* We may all view a product from a different point of view. Hence if your product possesses a property which others think is undesirable, you must reconstruct their world view so that they come to see that what you lack is no shortcoming and that what you have is an asset. For example, for a long time the Volkswagen did not have automatic transmission. Rather than admit that this was a shortcoming, they advertised from the point of view that standard gear shifts were really the greatest, and what "man" would want his car to drive him rather than vice versa? Further, anyone who has ever used contact paper, which is very useful, knows that in time it stretches. Rather than admit this, the company advertises that its product does not shrink. It all depends on how you look at it.

c) *classification:*   The important thing in classifying your product or products is to make sure that the classification is laudatory. For example, in my neighborhood delicatessen there are two sizes of precooked chickens: large and extra large. There is no such entity as a small or medium chicken. Another example of this kind of classification is found in eggs. Did you know that it is impossible to get a small egg? The smallest egg sold commercially is sold as a medium egg.

d) *definition:*   Suppose you were to read the word "champagne" on a bottle of wine. What would that tell you? To some people it means a wine from the Champagne region of France. Technically this is all that it means. Further, most of the wine from this region is sparkling, which means that bubbles form within it. Moreover, most of this wine is white. However, there are wines from Champagne which are red and some which are not sparkling. French champagne is rigidly produced and controlled, especially in labeling. An example of this is the fact that it is bottle fermented: the bubbles are allowed to form naturally in the bottle and not pumped in by some artificial device. This produces the best taste, but it is also very costly.

In America the law allows certain products to use the word "champagne," but the requirements are so loose that it is easy to buy an inferior product. A good many American champagnes are fermented not in the bottle, but in huge vats. If the champagne is vat fermented it must say "bulk process" on the label. However, this does not prevent some unscrupulous concern from saying "naturally fermented by bulk process." The word "natural" is almost a contradiction here, but the unscrupulous concern relies on the equivocation of meaning and the buyer's natural gullibility.

e) *analogy:* This is a widely used technique. It will be useful to recall our previous distinction between literal and figurative analogies. A literal analogy is a claim that if two things are alike in one or more respects, then they are alike in some further respect. A figurative analogy is just a dramatic device for emphasizing or explaining one point. A good deal of advertising relies upon the obscurity over this distinction. What are figurative analogies are presented as literal analogies. An American sports-type car, which is relatively inexpensive, is called the Ferrari of American cars. Ferrari is a prestigious automobile which is expensive and a masterpiece of technology. It may be that the only similarity (and certainly not an analogy) between the Ferrari and the American car is some slight styling feature. Yet advertising capitalizes upon this.

Another American automobile claims to be quieter inside than a Rolls Royce. This is probably true, but that is probably the beginning and the end of any superiority.

Driving home the conclusion:

Advertising does not rely upon complicated arguments. Its stock in trade is repetition. Of the devices it employs under this general head the most important are emotive language and the promise of residual benefits.

a) *residual benefits:* In his book *The Hidden Persuaders,* Vance Packard emphasizes the subliminal promise that goes along with each product. As one man put it, "The cosmetic manufacturers are not selling

lanolin, they are selling hope. . . . We do not buy just
an auto, we buy prestige." Although a bit overempha-
sized, there is a real point here. If a man does not feel
the need for an automobile it is not likely that you will
sell him one. On the other hand, given a man or market
for automobiles, and given competition which is very
similar technically to your product, some residual benefit must be offered. So you say that anyone can buy a
car of Brand X but if someone buys your brand or make
he not only gets a car but he gets a symbol of virility as
well. The connection between cars and sex cannot just
be invented by advertisers, there must already be some
connection in the minds of the audience. Sociologically
we may note that this particular connection between
cars and sex is the result of the fact that courtship
habits have changed a great deal over that past forty
years precisely because of the existence of cars.

b) *emotive language:* While we are on the subject of automobiles, we may note as an example of
emotive language the phrase "foreign midget" applied
to some cars made abroad. Foreign is descriptive
whereas the term "midget" refers to the generally small
size of foreign cars. "Midget," however, carries the negative connotation of something abnormal, yet given
conditions in foreign lands (and even in many places in
America) the small car might be more rational.

The greatest example of emotive language, so
clever that it is almost unbelievable, is an advertisement
not for any specific product, but for "Brand Names." It
simply says you can rely upon Brand Names. Here you
are being conditioned to respond to advertising itself or
to conditioning itself. Amazing!

Some brands have actually achieved a kind of

superstatus. Scotch tape is not just a brand in the popular mind, but has become the generic term used by consumers of cellophane tape. With such emotive status it is unlikely that competitors will have any chance. We can all learn a great deal from advertising.

CHAPTER TWO

Attacking an Argument

There are two main reasons for learning techniques of attacking arguments. First, one can build a stronger case for his own position if, in addition to presenting positive considerations for it, he shows that there are serious weaknesses in the arguments for its rivals. Remember, in this connection, that few positions of practical importance can be *conclusively proved;* thus, while you are not likely to be able to *prove* your own position, you can make it look very good indeed by punching holes in the arguments of the opposition.

Second, once you have mastered the art of offense you will undoubtedly become more sophisticated in defense of your original position. Anticipating what and where the attacks against you will originate and how they might progress is half the battle.

AUDIENCE REACTION

For the sake of discussion we shall assume that someone else has already presented his case and now you are called upon to attack it. Before you do anything else you *must* gauge audience reaction to the original

71

presentation of your opponent's case. There are three general possible reactions: (1) either your opponent has been successful in varying degrees in persuading the audience to adopt his point of view; or (2) the audience remains undecided; or (3) your opponent has been unsuccessful in varying degrees in getting the audience to accept his case.

Let us discuss general strategy with respect to these three possibilities, reversing the order of consideration. If your opponent has been unsuccessful, the first thing you must do is to pinpoint precisely those spots in his presentation which were weakest and least successful with the audience. Then concentrate most of your fire on these spots, thereby reinforcing in the minds of the audience the weakness of his position and your brilliance in sharing their perceptiveness. Here you are combining a critique of the opposition with flattery of the audience. Next, when you feel that the audience is with you, you may proceed to employ the techniques and rules to be discussed below and you may do so with humor and ridicule. Please note: *humor and ridicule are effective* against an opponent *only if you know yourself to be preeminent* in the eyes of the present audience. Otherwise you will offend all concerned.

There are two special devices which should be used in a blatant manner in those cases where you are sure that your opponent has been unsuccessful. Those devices are the *ad hominem* attack and the genetic fallacy.

Ad hominem:

To attack *ad hominem* is to attack the man who presents an argument rather than the argument itself. There are some subtle variations of it which you will discover throughout this chapter, but here we are concerned only with its more blatant use. There are two occasions during a discussion when you may use it: either after you have demolished the argument by independent means, or in those cases where your opponent's argument has been so unsuccessful with the audience that it is not worth demolishing. This is important. There are no doubt, as you shall see, all sorts of clever things you can do, but these things should be done only if needed to win. If you can win without using a technique, do not use it. You may distract both yourself and the audience.

There are various ways of attacking a man. You might begin by chastising him for insulting the intelligence of the audience by offering such a shabby case. Or you may explain why he has adopted such a foolish view.

Examples of *ad hominem* include the following. When asked to debate a particular subject with his students, a teacher may reply that he does not discuss such serious matters with a bunch of ignoramuses. Or a speaker invited to the campus by students may refuse to answer the questions of his academic audience by noting that they have not read a particular writer or have not read a particular book or magazine article. Or we might hear that pollution is just a shadow issue to distract our attention from either *(a)* antiwar protests or *(b)* the Communist conspiracy.

Genetic fallacy:

The most sophisticated form of *ad hominem* is a special kind of counterargument itself, namely the genetic fallacy. To explain genetically is to describe the origin of an event, process, thing, etc. It is a kind of historical account of how things got that way. Usually it is employed in a diagnostic manner, thereby implying that you are discussing the case history of a disease.

Genetic explanations are certainly valid and useful in other contexts, but they are especially useful in undermining an opponent.

Perhaps the two most famous uses of genetic explanation are Freudian psychoanalysis and various forms of Marxism. The anxieties, neuroses, and psychoses of many patients are identified as the result of a course of development which began in childhood. Usually some traumatic experience in childhood is the cause of the neurosis. For example, being locked in a closet as punishment might "cause" claustrophobia, or being inculcated with the view that sex is dirty might "cause" one to be frigid or impotent or require elaborate masochistic devices to relieve sexual tension. Marxists can explain, so they claim, not only the history of economic development, but why it exhibits certain patterns, such as boom and bust, and why some workers feel alienated in the capitalist system. In addition, both Freudians and Marxists can explain why some people do not accept their theories. Anyone who refuses to see that sex is all pervasive reveals a symptom of Victorian sexual repression. Perhaps he has an Oedipus complex and seeks to hide it by denying its existence in anyone. Anyone who does not support the Communist party is a tool of capitalist repression. To oppose such theories is to expose oneself to public scorn in some circles.

Genetic explanations abound in common popular argumentation. The contempt of the business world for the academic world is explained as the awareness that "those who can, do; those who cannot, teach." The contempt of the academic world for the business world is explained as the awareness that business is part of the establishment which is necessarily repressive and status quo oriented. Adolescents simply cannot speak to anyone over twenty-five. Age functions here as a genetic explanation of political, social, and cultural blindness. All rebellious youth are to be dismissed as the result of permissive parents. Given a sympathetic audience, you can always find some explanation as to why the opposition is so stupid and save yourself the trouble of having to deal logically with its arguments.

We come now to the second possibility, namely, where the audience is still undecided. Here you should avoid using most of the techniques mentioned above. Instead you should once more try to discover which points in your opponent's presentation were strongest and which were weakest. If you can combat the strong ones, then do so; if not, simply act as if they were never mentioned. In any case, the weak points should be exploited. The exact anatomy of proceeding to do so will be discussed shortly.

The third possibility is what to do if your opponent has been successful. To begin with, *moral posturing* calculated to shame your opponent and audience is *very effective when you are the obvious underdog* in a dispute. Now if your opponent's success is owing to *his* use of techniques of deception such as those we are discussing, you can probably win points by exposing this fact and accusing him (more or less gently) of being a trickster. But if your audience is so dimwitted that it would not see what you are driving at, you should stick to using the deceptive tricks yourself. Above all, do not be so harsh with your opponent as to increase the audience's sympathy for him, and do not give the appearance yourself of being crafty or nit-picking. Most audiences immediately dislike someone who seems impressed with his ability to argue, so avoid looking oppressively flashy or pleased with your incisiveness or wit. Strive to look like a slightly wounded, unjustly used underdog, but again, don't overdo it. Know your audience!

If your audience is somewhat sophisticated, but perhaps taken in by your opponent's skillful presentation, then you should expose him as a sophist and a trickster who is insulting the intelligence of the audience. You then engage in a point by point critique of his tricks. Finally, after the exposé you claim that you *shall not stoop* to using such dishonest means.

ANATOMY OF REFUTATION

We come now to the anatomy of refutation, the means whereby we undermine the case of the opposition. Remember, all of your opponent's arguments can be shown to be defective. It is simply a question of your ingenuity and persistence. I shall begin by diagramming the form of attack, then exemplify some of the diagram's general principles, and then launch into a detailed analysis of specific refutation procedures.

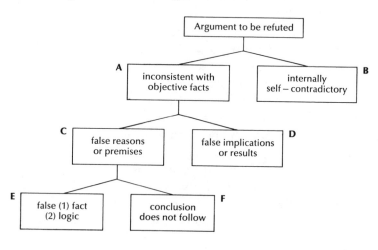

Every argument consists of a major point or conclusion supported by premises or reasons which allegedly provide evidence for that conclusion. When attacking an argument we are claiming one of two things, or perhaps both: an argument is defective (1) when the evidence contradicts the conclusion, or (2) when the evidence is simply false or inadequate. Since A above will be subdivided, let us examine B above first.

B: An argument is internally self-contradictory either when one of the premises contradicts the conclusion or the premises contradict each other. For example, if I claim that Fidel cigars are better than all others because they are so high priced that only a few men can buy them, and, at the same time, that they are the largest selling cigar, then I have made contradictory claims. You cannot claim that something is good because it is exclusive and claim that something is good because it is popular at the same time.

A: An argument may be inconsistent with objective fact when either C the premises or reasons appealed to are simply false, or D the implications or results of the conclusion would be considered false. An example of the latter would be an argument which began with information about pollution and ecology and then concluded with a condemnation of all technology as being harmful to life. The false implications of this position are apparent in that a great deal of modern medicine which preserves and serves life is the result of technology. Surely we would not want to reject that.

C: Reasons or premises are false or unacceptable either when F the conclusion does not follow, or E we can simply show the premises to be false. In the case of F we say the argument is a non sequitur. This differs from the case of B because in B we have a contradiction, whereas in the case of F there is no connection at all. For example, one may argue to the conclusion that Americans as a whole have greater innate intelligence now than they did forty years ago because there are more Americans attending college now than ever before. This is to offer a reason which is true but totally irrelevant to the conclusion. There is no direct connection between innate intelligence and attendance at a college. The colleges may have lowered their standards or expanded facilities for reasons having nothing to do with the intelligence of applicants.

E: A reason or premise can be seen to be false in either a direct or indirect way. In a direct way, if someone claims that it is raining we might show that he is wrong directly by looking outside, etc. A reason or premise may be shown to be false indirectly in a number of ways.

Let us consider the argument that eighteen-year-olds should be allowed to vote. Let us further suppose that the sole reason or premise offered is that liability to the draft should be the sole determining factor in giving the right to vote. Usually it is stated in some highly emotional form like "conscription without representation is tyranny."

The first way of attacking this premise is to (1) add another premise which is known to be true, and (2) then derive a false conclusion. Obviously this invalidates the premise. For example, girls are not subject to the draft so we would have to exclude them from the vote. Obviously being subject to the draft cannot be the sole determinant in voting.

The second way of attacking this premise is to derive another conclusion which would be inconsistent with the given conclusion or some other your opponent may draw. For example, if the draft age were lowered to sixteen, then sixteen-year-olds (or twelve-year-olds, or whatever the draft age is) would have the right to vote. But your opponent has argued that voting should begin at age eighteen. The same sort of inconsistent conclusion would work with a voluntary army. Then no one but the volunteers would have the right to vote.

A third general method of attacking this premise is to show that it is a generalization with known exceptions, hence it is unacceptable. Liability to the draft is no present criterion for voting since men over thirty-five, who are obviously not subject to the draft, have the right to vote. Voting then depends on some other criterion or criteria. All of this is not to say that eighteen-year-olds should not have the right to vote. The refutation only shows that liability to the draft is not the premise or reason which can be used.

Refutation of Pity Appeals.

The appeal to pity, like the appeals to authority, *ad populum*, and precedents, is largely an attempt to gain the sympathy of the audience. If any of these appeals has been successful, then it is important to realize that the audience has a certain sympathy for that kind of argument. Hence the refutation follows one of two patterns: either we invoke a higher order appeal of the same nature, or we attempt to turn the tables.

If your opponent has appealed to pity, then you should act as if his example of pity is a general premise. Then add some premise of your own which you think would be accepted by the audience and derive a conclusion inconsistent with your opponent's. For example, suppose your opponent has argued that we should destroy all atomic weapons and began his argument with a detailed survey of the consequences of Hiroshima. Further we suppose the appeal to pity to have been an effective one. The audience obviously feels pity for those who suffer. The only way to counter this appeal is to point out that if America had not possessed or used atomic weapons on Japan (as your opponent argues), and if the war had had to be concluded by an invasion of the Japanese islands, then (adding the supplementary premise) by the best estimates the casualties on both sides, including military and civilian, would have been astronomical. Now add: How many Japanese and American children are able to know their parents, as well as themselves, to be alive because of that courageous decision to drop the bomb? The use of atomic weapons actually minimized suffering.

As a second example, imagine a lawyer defending a juvenile client by claiming that *because* his client is a child, *therefore* we ought to make allowances. The appeal to pity has the following structure: because of *x*, therefore *y*.

We turn the tables by deriving a different conclusion from the same premise: because of *x*, therefore not *y*. Because he is a child, we ought not to make allowances, otherwise we shall be establishing or encouraging a bad habit.

Refutation of Authority.

There are two ways of undermining your opponent's use of authority, either by an *ad hominem* attack on his specific authorities, or by providing counter-authorities. Further, there are at least six different kinds of *ad hominem* attacks upon an authority.

First, if a man is quoted as an authority and at the same time is known to have opinions that are inconsistent with the appeals to pity, *ad populum,* or precedent used by your opponent, then you should pounce upon this inconsistency. Let us go back to a previous example. If your opponent has argued against the stockpiling of nuclear weapons, and further has exemplified his case by the pity appeal of Hiroshima, and in addition calls in as an authority on the effects of nuclear blasts a scientist or military analyst, then do the following. If the military analyst or scientist is an expert on the consequences of the disaster following a nuclear blast and at the same time is in favor of stockpiling nuclear weapons, then you should obtain this admission quickly. If the very expert employed by your opponent does not share his ultimate conclusion, then you have really embarrassed the opposition.

Second, if the alleged expert belongs to a group or espouses a cause to which you know the audience is opposed or hostile, then undermine the authority by the use of guilt by association. Surely, anyone belonging to questionable organizations is not a trustworthy authority. For example, if a policeman is accused of shooting an unarmed Black man and a ballistics expert is called in to testify that the bullet was fired from that policeman's revolver, then check to see what groups the ballistics expert belongs to. If, for example, he contributes regularly to the NAACP and you are dealing with a racist audience or jury, then invoke this information in order to cast doubt on the honesty of the analysis done by the expert.

Third, an expert may be undermined by pointing out the distinction between theory and practice. Lots of things sound great in theory, such as how the computer is here to save us, and then are complete flops in practice. For example, in trying to obtain public support for a space program many experts were called upon to tell of the benefits of the research that go on in such a program. Some of these benefits have not actually taken place. Many were based upon theoretical presuppositions which could easily be attacked. Moreover, in dealing with human problems we are usually flooded with imbecilic theories about how to solve these problems, and we all know how many of these proposed solutions have failed. Moreover, we all know that the experts produced by our opponent are people who live in ivory towers (i.e., they teach at colleges or universities) which are far removed from reality.

Fourth, any authority who deals with extreme abstractions can be undermined by stressing the distinction between theory and fact. The public is frequently unaware of this distinction as the press indiscriminately reports all scientific statements as if they were facts. Many of them are purely theoretical. For example, can anyone, no matter how intelligent, really explain the beginning of the universe? If there were a beginning, then something must have preceded it. All theories rely upon some pre-existing event or thing or state like an expanding gas, etc. This is not literally a beginning of the universe if something was already there. Besides, could we ever check such an event? Moreover, the history of science abounds with great scientists who believed false if not idiotic things. Galileo, for example, wanted to explain tides in terms of the sun. This is a little difficult to work out especially with tides at night! Kepler, despite his genius, had a whole collection of bizarre beliefs about number mysticism. Many men have made their reputations by proposing theories which were later discarded.

Fifth, if you are at a loss as to how an authority may be undermined you might always try quoting him out of context. For example, supposed that in defense of the American involvement in Indochina, our opponent invokes the late President Eisenhower as a supporter and appeals to his authority on foreign policy matters. You can counter by examining a number of Eisenhower speeches and seeing if you can find a statement that might be used against your opponent. With a little ingenuity you can. Eisenhower once said that if elections were held (this was during his administration) in Vietnam tomorrow, the Vietcong would win because they were prepared to use terror tactics to get their way. By deftly ignoring the qualification about Vietcong terror, you may then quote Eisenhower as agreeing that the people of South Vietnam really want to be governed by the Vietcong, and this obviously is inconsistent with stated policy and your opponent's case. Of course you are not quoting the whole context, but remember you are quoting something and most people are too lazy to look up the original statement.

Sixth, as a last ditch tactic against any expert you should engage in a general attack on all expertise. Here you can discount or dismiss an expert's knowledge by appealing to a more general truth. Suppose you are dealing with an alleged medical expert whose testimony is not to your liking. You may point out that knowledge in general is highly uncertain. And if knowledge in general is uncertain, then surely some particular kind of alleged knowledge, even medical knowledge, is uncertain. Finally, you might even hint at the fact that there is a conspiracy among all of your opponent's experts, especially if they agree.

The other general form of attack against expertise and authority is to provide counter-experts. Here too there are two possibilities. First, if you feel that you have been successful in undermining the confidence of the audience in your opponent's experts, then introduce your own experts who will support your case. Second, if you had to use the sixth method outlined above—a general critique of all authority and expertise—then introduce counter-experts not necessarily as supports for your case, but simply for effect. Surely if all of these experts disagree, what is the use of using experts at all! Ridicule is the final weapon here. For examples, I suggest that you consult any discussion among experts on how to raise children.

Refutation of Ad Populum.

Ad populum appeals by their very nature are very popular. The major ploy against them is to invoke another *ad populum* which supports your case and/or goes against the case of your opponent, one which you think might have an even greater appeal. For example, in redistricting or in choosing candidates it is frequently suggested that minority groups be placed into a stronghold or given a candidate with the same cultural background in order to guarantee them some kind of representation. This seems to be consistent with a democratic attempt to do justice to all legitimate interest groups within the society and is thus an *ad populum* appeal. To counter it you might point out that such a system gives the minority a voice but little power, since any one representative may be ignored. In the tenth Federalist paper, James Madison argued for another ideal which is also part of the American political system of ideals, namely the notion that a political representative should be encouraged by redistricting and other means to represent a wide variety of interests. In fact, by having a representative for a specific interest group we are encouraging factionalism which is just the evil we want to avoid. Here we have attempted to undermine one *ad populum* appeal by another which we believe to have a greater appeal.

There is a second way of attacking your opponent's use of the *ad populum* appeal. This way is to be used only if you cannot think of an effective counter *ad populum* appeal. What you must then do is engage in a general attack on *ad populum* appeals. You must point out to your audience the extent to which what most people accept is wrong. You can drive this point home by giving examples such as the fact that many people once believed that the earth was flat, and surely the majority opinion here was wrong. In the realm of values, which is more appropriate to the *ad populum* appeal, we may note that the charging of interest (usury) was once frowned upon, whereas today a vibrant economy is impossible without a credit system that depends upon charging interest.

A variation of the foregoing theme is to appeal to a value which is at once at odds with the general *ad populum* position but nevertheless shared by the narrow interests of your audience. For instance, although democracy or majority rule is part of our general *ad populum* repertory, when dealing with intellectuals in general and academics in particular you may appeal to élitism, the belief that only superior people (presumably those attached to higher education) should be allowed to make major decisions. Here derision of what the masses believe in is most appropriate and persuasive.

Refutation of Precedent.

The obvious refutation of an appeal to precedent is to invoke a counterprecedent. For example, in the Supreme Court case of *Keswick vs. Buick* (1937), we discover that Mr. Keswick was injured and disabled by an accident he suffered because of his recently purchased Buick automobile. It was later substantiated that the Buick was defective. Mr. Keswick sued. In its defense, the Buick lawyers argued that they should not be held responsible for the defective Buick on the grounds that such liability would economically undermine Buick in particular and the whole economy in general. Here the precedent is the security of the free enterprise system. Mr. Keswick's lawyers argued that his disability prevented him from earning a living and thereby from supporting his family. Here the counterprecedent is the preservation of the institution of the family. Mr. Keswick won.

The second way of attacking a precedent is to show that is does not apply to the case at hand because of the presence of extenuating circumstances or significant differences. Let us imagine a shipwreck and the survivors on a lifeboat far off the beaten path. Further, there are too many survivors for the small lifeboat and in addition there is a storm coming up. In order for some to survive, the occupants of the lifeboat must row some 1,500 miles to the nearest land. By precedent the captain should try to save everybody and in order of preference women and children should be saved first. The captain violated the precedent, first by not allowing everyone into the lifeboat, thereby causing some to perish by drowning, and second by excluding everyone other than able-bodied men and women. He was tried for murder and dereliction of duty. His defense was that precedent did not apply to his case because of extenuating circumstances. If he had followed precedent, all of them would have perished. Doing what he did, at least some were able to survive.

The third way of criticizing a precedent is to show what happens when a precedent is extended to its extreme. For example, democratic procedure is a fine precedent but inappropriate in some cases. Imagine if we had elections to determine who should purify the city water supply or how it should be purified. This should be a matter of expertise and chemistry, not democracy. As a final example, to justify the use of violence on the grounds that there is a precedent for it is to base a case on shaky grounds. Anyone can invoke that precedent, including a lynch mob.

Refutation of Statistics.

To begin with, one may attack the particular statistical evidence offered by an opponent in the presentation of his case. That evidence or information may simply be false. On the other hand, it may be true information but incorrectly interpreted.

How does one correctly interpret statistical evidence? To begin with, we use statistical evidence only when we cannot get at something directly. For example, I cannot directly examine tomorrow's weather, but I can present statistical evidence for what I think it might be. What I want to know about may be an individual object, person, event (tomorrow's weather), etc., or it may be about a whole collection of things (all the swans in the world). The group of things being examined is called the *population* and the portion that I directly examine is called the sample. When we draw a conclusion about the population based upon the sample we are making a statistical inference. If the inference is to be of any help, then the sample must be unbiased or unloaded. Another way of putting it is that the sample must be *random* in the sense that it represents a cross section of the whole of the population.

The most devastating blow that can be delivered

against statistical evidence is the claim that it is not a random sample, i.e., that the sample is biased or unrepresentative. The most famous example of this is the *Literary Digest* presidential poll of 1936. We have all come to accept the general reliability of computers which on the basis of one percent of the vote in Oshkosh can predict a whole national election. However this was not always the case, especially in less sophisticated days. By polling people selected from a telephone directory and then calling them, the pollsters for the *Literary Digest* predicted that Alfred Landon would defeat Franklin Roosevelt handily. The sample consisted of over two million telephone calls. As we know, Roosevelt overwhelmed Landon 523 to 8 electoral votes. The sample, although large, was biased because it relied upon people who could afford a telephone during the Depression. Many of Roosevelt's supporters did not own telephones.

The trick to use here is to declare, no matter what, that your opponent's statistics are not based upon a random sample. Find a factor, any factor, and claim that the factor is crucial and has been overlooked. Here a little ingenuity will be required on your part. Keep searching until you find some factor that has been overlooked, regardless of whether it is really important, and keep harping on it. Some examples follow:

Is the sample representative in *time?* (You can always say that last year's statistics are out of date.)

Is the sample representative in *space?* (Did you interview people on the first floor, the second floor, basements, etc.? This may seem irrelevant, but who is to say for sure?)

Is the sample representative *economically?*

Is the sample representative *geographically?* (People in the Bible Belt? People in Eastern urban areas?).

Is the sample representative by *sex*? By *marital status*?

Is the sample representative by *age*?

In short, there are an infinite number of possibilities which might be relevant and which, therefore, might be exploited. Needless to add, if you are aware of some factor that has been ignored and to which you know your audience is sympathetic, then pounce upon that one.

The same technique of emphasizing a missing crucial factor may be used in attacking any graphs or charts used. Supplying the missing factor or factors, if possible, may enable you either to undermine the graphs presented or to present contrary graphs. We shall see more of this shortly.

The second way of attacking your opponent's statistics is to present a different set of statistics which controverts the original set. At the very least, this has the effect of neutralizing any advantage he may have gained from his initial presentation; if you have successfully challenged his statistics in a manner outlined above, then your counterstatistical evidence will prevail. For example, in order to counter one poll you may present evidence of your own poll that supports your contention. Rival political candidates frequently sponsor private polls in order to persuade potential supporters and voters that they, the candidates, are really out in front and therefore potential winners.

An especially important kind of counterstatistic is not one that contradicts the original set (your poll shows Smith is leading, your opponent's poll shows that Jones is leading), but one that supplements the original set in such a way that a different conclusion must be drawn. For example, owners of businesses (management) may point out that wages have risen at a high rate among their employees. This may very well be true. At the same time, you may present counterstatistics showing that the cost of living has risen at a staggering rate. Hence the real purchasing power of the employees' wages may be much less than at the lower wage. This kind of counterstatistic is very effective in combatting an illicit or misleading comparison. When the opposition has used a graph to present its misleading comparison, a countergraph incorporating the new statistic should be used.

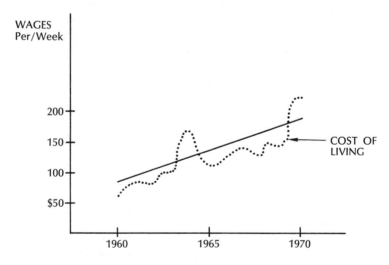

In the above graph, we assume that the opposition (employers) presented the original solid line graph, and we (the union) have superimposed the dotted line of the cost of living to show the "true" state of things.

When presenting counterstatistics you may be able to supplement them by an *ad hominem* argument as well. For example, if your opponent did not know about the existence of the counterstatistics, then you may imply that he is a fool who has not carefully researched his case. This tends to undermine the confidence of the audience in the rest of his argument as well. If your opponent is aware of the counterstatistics and he did not mention them, then you may imply that he is a scoundrel (or worse, a liar) who is deceiving the audience by suppressing relevant information. Since nobody can present every piece of information, you can always use this technique. If you are sure that the audience is with you, keep asking as a rhetorical question, "Why wasn't this information mentioned?"

If you cannot find a flaw in your opponent's statistics and if you cannot present counterstatistics, then you must engage in a general attack on the use of statistics itself. You can do this by first mentioning to your audience that every sophisticated person knows that statistical information may be misused. This is true. You then proceed to exemplify some cases of how statistics are misused.

To begin with, statistical information is information about a class of people, items, events, things, etc. It is not really information about any individual person, item, event, thing, etc. Hence it is always possible that what is true of the group is not necessarily true of any individual member of that group. To say that the average American family has 2.5 children is not to say that the Smith family next door has 2.5 children. Such a state of affairs, anyway, is literally impossible. The fact that drivers under twenty-five are, statistically speaking, a greater insurance risk does not mean that every driver under twenty-five is reckless.

If your opponent has presented statistical evidence about an individual you can always construct some evidence to prove the opposite. For example, suppose your opponent is trying to prove that Smith is a criminal type and offers the following statistical argument:

Seventy-five percent of slum dwellers are criminal types.

Smith is a slum dweller.

Therefore, it is highly probable that Smith is a criminal type. To counter this argument and to show how ridiculous it is to use statistics, you present the following statistical argument:

One percent of all Jehovah's Witnesses are criminal types.

Smith is a Jehovah's Witness.

Therefore, it is highly improbable that Smith is a criminal type.

Your second example should be used to show that any attempt to draw conclusions from statistical evidence about the future, a process known as *extrapolation,* is risky if not impossible. Such extrapolation must be based upon the assumption that there will be no changes in circumstances and that the process being described statistically has no implications for itself. To predict the cost of living for five years from now is silly without taking into account what reaction the President or the Federal Reserve Board might have if the cost of living should rise or fall drastically. Perhaps the best example of how silly extrapolation is comes from Mark Twain, who wrote the following in *Life on the Mississippi:*

In the space of 176 years the Lower Mississippi has shortened itself 242 miles. This is an average of a trifle over one mile and a third per year. Therefore, any calm person, who is not blind or idiotic, can see that in the Old Oolithic Silurian period, just a million years ago next November, the

Lower Mississippi River was upwards of one million three
hundred thousand miles long, and stuck out over the Gulf of
Mexico like a fishing rod. And by the same token any person
can see that 742 years from now the Lower Mississippi will
be only a mile and three quarters long, and Cairo and New
Orleans will have joined their streets together, and be plod-
ding comfortably along under a single mayor and a mutual
board of alderman. There is something fascinating about science. One gets such wholesome returns of conjecture out of
such a trifling investment of fact.

The third example of the futility of statistics is
traditionally known as the *gambler's fallacy*. As we all
know, the flipping of a normal coin leads either to a
head up or to a tail coming up. These are the only two
possibilities. Thus there is a probability of one in two
that heads will turn up. The result is called a chance
event. Of course, in two flips the chance of a head turning up twice is one in four, and so on. Suppose a gambler is betting on either heads or tails and suppose
further that heads has turned up five times in a row.
Since he has misunderstood the probability theory the
gambler may think that the probability of tails coming
up after the run of heads is very great, certainly greater
than one in two. He bets on tails and loses. The fallacy
is in believing that the run of a chance event (heads
five times in a row) alters the probability of that event
(heads) in the future. Each flip of the coin is an independent event uninfluenced by past occurrences. With
each flip the probability remains the same one in two.
This brings me to the final refutation of using statistics
at all. Why should we believe that the chance of heads
or tails is one in two? Did you ever try flipping a coin
to see what happens? Try it ten times and see. (Here

you might perform it for your audience and hope to get a six and four or a seven and three combination of heads and tails. If it does not work in ten tries, try twenty, and so on until the results are significantly uneven.)

Refutation of Theoretical Constructs.

Most people distrust abstractions. Hence, in order to undermine the use of abstractions and theoretical constructs in the arguments of your opponent, you must first point out that such abstractions exist. For example, if your opponent analyzes the behavior or motivation of someone in terms of the Freudian unconscious or subconscious, you must point out that these are abstract terms. Second, no abstract term, by definition, can refer to a thing or things which are directly observable. This is where audience distrust is to be exploited. Point out how impossible it is to identify the unconscious, thereby giving the impression that the thing really does not exist. For example, where would one find the unconscious or the subconscious? Under the left armpit? In the little finger? In the brain?

A further difficulty with theoretical constructs or abstractions is the fact that they are rarely clearly defined as to their nature, that is, whether they are things, processes, events, etc. Take the Marxist term "bourgeois." How does one recognize a member of the bourgeoisie? Is it automatically by membership in the economic setup? Would an assembly-line worker for the Ford company who owns some stock in the company be considered a member of the bourgeoisie or the proletariat? Moreover, Marx claimed that some members of the bourgeoisie could rise above it at the same time he claimed that being a member prevented one from seeing any other social ideology but his own.

The same kind of analysis can be given of the term "Establishment." Those who use it simply do not define or show us how to identify what they are talking about. Once the opposition admits that they are not talking about an observable entity but providing a speculative framework, then you have successfully isolated and made benign this part of their argument. The burden of proof will have to be supplied by the rest of what they say.

Refutation of Classification.

In giving a critique of someone else's classification you are doing so for the benefit of the audience. Hence it is important to keep in mind the audience's point of view. The first way of undermining a classification is to find an exception. Exceptions are of two kinds: either something that does not fit at all, or something that fits in more than one place. For example, suppose someone argues that there have been no great American poets in the twentieth century. You offer as a counterexample T. S. Eliot. Your opponent replies that Eliot was a British citizen. Here you must rely upon your audience. If the audience considers Eliot an American you should press the point that the classification of great poets must include Eliot and hence your opponent's classification of great poets fails to account for something.

Eliot can serve as an example of the second kind of problem. Suppose someone is classifying poets by nationality. Is Eliot to be classified as an American or as a Britisher? He was born an American but later became a British subject. W. H. Auden was born a Britisher and is now an American citizen. He might easily fit both categories and hence foul up the classification again.

The second kind of objection to any classification is

that it fails to serve any purpose, especially the purpose for which it was intended. For example, it is commonplace to distinguish between dictatorships of the right (which are always called dictatorships) and dictatorships of the left (which are rarely if ever called dictatorships). In fact, the right-left distinction in general is widely used. However, does it really serve any purpose to make this distinction? The rationale behind it is that dictatorships of the left are supposed to be progressive and verging ultimately toward democracy, whereas dictatorships of the right are supposed to be reactionary. In fact, this is a false distinction. Can one really see a difference in the daily life between Spain and Albania? If the classification is made economically (Marxist variety) it is said that the "right" supports capitalism whereas the "left" favors socialism. Have you noticed that the latest Peruvian junta has moved to nationalize American-owned industries? Is a military junta in Peru to be considered leftist?

Refutation of Definition.

If your opponent offers a nonstandard definition, then there are two things you can do. First you should point out that the definition he used is nonstandard. If your audience is annoyed by nonstandard definitions, then engage in a supplementary *ad hominem* at once. Either he is a fool who does not know what words mean, or he is a scoundrel trying to put one over on everybody.

If mere exposure does not work, then try a second kind of attack. Usually an odd definition is an attempt to make something true by definition. If this is so, then expose your opponent as offering a *circular argument* or *petito principi*. Suppose your opponent is trying to prove the existence of God and offers the following argument:

The Bible is the word of God.
The Bible says that God exists.
Therefore, God exists.

The evidence for the existence of God is a set of statements in the Bible. When questioned as to why we should believe the Bible, our opponent argues that (1) God, by definition, is truthful, and (2) the Bible is, by definition, the word of God. Now, even if I accept the first definition there is no reason why I should accept the second one. If I did not already believe in God, I would hardly accept as evidence the definition that the Bible is the word of God. The argument is circular in that it assumes what it is trying to prove. We also say that the argument is question begging since it begs (assumes) the very thing it is trying to prove. The whole controversy thus hinges upon the definition.

Refutation of Analogies.

As we noted before, there are two kinds of analogies, literal and figurative. In the case of literal analogies one argues that similarities in several crucial respects implies similarity in some one other respect. Since all analogies can only be partial, the refutation of a literal analogy depends upon finding one or more features which differ between the two things being compared and to press the point that it is this difference or differences which are crucial.

Suppose someone were to argue that all children could become geniuses if only their diet were improved. As evidence for this thesis he offers an analogy between physical growth and diet on the one hand and intellectual (mental) growth and diet on the other. Studies have shown that an improved diet leads to physical growth and even increases in height. Moreover, with a better breakfast, children performed better in school.

Where does this literal analogy break down? First, there is a crucial difference in ages at which nervous system development takes place. While physical growth goes on continuously until maturity, the brain is already 90 percent complete by the age of four. Second, there is no correlation of brain size and intelligence. Third, and most important, no diet can make a person with a small frame (determined genetically) into a seven-footer. Analogously (here we refute one analogy with another), although a better diet may help us all to improve our mental functioning, it cannot make us into geniuses.

A figurative analogy, as opposed to a literal analogy, is meant only to highlight dramatically some point in the argument. The most effective way of combatting this sort of device is to take the same metaphor or analogy used by your opponent and to arrive at a different or the opposite conclusion. This technique, when successfully applied, is a mild form of ridicule or amusement. It also leaves the audience with the impression that you have either bested your opponent in argumentation or you are, at the very least, more clever than he is.

As an example let us take one of the traditional arguments for the nature and existence of God, the so-called argument from design. It is argued that God is the principle of order in the universe and that by studying the nature of that order or regularity we may infer something about what God is like. This argument and analogy were successfully refuted by the eighteenth century British philosopher David Hume, in his *Dialogues Concerning Natural Religion:*

> But were this world ever so perfect a production, it must still remain uncertain, whether all of the excellences of the work [world] can justly be ascribed to the workman [God]. If we survey a ship, what an exalted idea must we form of the ingenuity of the carpenter, who framed so complicated, useful, and beautiful a machine? And what surprise must we entertain, when we find him a stupid mechanic, who imitated others, and copied an art, which, through a long succession of ages, after multiplied trials, mistakes, corrections, deliberations, and controversies, had been gradually improving? Many worlds might have been botched and bungled, throughout an eternity, ere this system was struck out: Much labor lost: Many fruitless trials made: And a slow, but continued improvement carried on during infinite ages in the art of world-making. In such subjects, who can determine, where the truth; nay, who can conjecture where the probability, lies; amidst a great number of hypotheses which may be proposed, and a still greater number which may be imagined?
>
> And what shadow of an argument . . . can you produce, from your hypothesis, to prove the unity of the Deity? A great number of men join in building a house or a ship, in rearing a city, in framing a commonwealth: Why may not several Deities combine in contriving and framing a world? This is only so much greater similarity to human affairs. By sharing the work among several, we may so much farther limit the attributes of each, and get rid of that extensive power and knowledge, which must be supposed in one Deity, and which, according to you, can only serve to weaken the proof of his existence. And if such foolish, such vicious creatures as man can yet often unite in framing and executing one plan; how much more those Deities or Daemons, whom we may suppose several degrees more perfect?

. . . men are mortal, and renew their species by generation. . . . Why must this circumstance, so universal, so essential, be excluded from those numerous and limited Deities? And why not become a perfect anthropomorphite? Why not assert the Deity or Deities to be corporeal, and to have eyes, a nose, mouth, ears, etc.?

In a word . . . a man, who follows your hypothesis, is able, perhaps, to assert, or conjecture, that the universe, sometime, arose from something like a design: But beyond that position he cannot ascertain one single circumstance. . . . This world, for aught he knows . . . was only the first rude essay of some infant Deity, who afterwards abandoned it, ashamed of his lame performance; it is the work only of some dependent, inferior Deity; and is the object of derision to his superiors: it is the production of old age and dotage in some superannuated Deity, and ever since his death, has run on at adventures. . . .

ATTACKING THE CONCLUSION

So far we have concentrated on offsetting your opponent's attempt to provide a favorable audience reaction and we have attempted specific refutations of the building blocks he needed to arrive at his conclusion. It is now time to examine the conclusion.

Before actually demolishing the conclusion you should try to make your audience realize that you have exposed cracks in the brittle structure offered by your opponent. So you should begin by offering a general characterization of your opponent's argument.

Summarize what you take to be the case of your opponent, but in order to clarify the case for the audience you should engage in a little translation so as to put that case in as bad a light as possible. Take the words used by your opponent and try to substitute those which will have a negative connotation in the mind of the audience. Below are a few examples of such translation.

discriminate	=	prejudice
alteration	=	radical innovation
existing order	=	antiquated prejudice
protective custody	=	thrown into a dungeon
religious zeal	=	fanaticism
law and order	=	political repression

In addition, you should be as picayune as possible by picking on his actual words rather than his meaning. This task will be made especially easy for you if your opponent takes the trouble of trying to make his presentation a little stylized or literary. For example, if he talks about the economy and mentions the mysteries of the stock market, you should pick him up on the word "mystery" and declare that you are not interested in mysteries or detective stories, thereby implying that he does not know what he is talking about.

Finally, in offering a general characterization of someone else's argument, you should dismiss it or categorize it emotively in terms of some generally known position that is rejected by your audience. Thus with some audiences an entire position might be dismissed as Marxist malarky, outmoded idealism, old-fashioned liberalism, racist, or irrelevant.

After a general characterization of the argument, you should attack the route taken by your opponent to his conclusion. Here you are criticizing the means he used to go from the evidence to the conclusion. Whether or not he is guilty of them, you can accuse him of certain traditional formal fallacies. Moreover, where possible, you should use the *Latin names* of these fallacies because this will make the audience believe you are skilled in identifying such fallacies and because the error sounds so much worse, just like a rare disease, when described in Latin.

Hasty Generalization.

If your opponent has used statistical information or particular facts of any kind to arrive at a generalization, then you should claim that the generalization was too hasty. This can be done in one of two ways. Either you provide evidence of an exception to his generalization, or argue that he did not examine enough cases even if you cannot think of a counterinstance. A variation of this argument is the claim that no adequate sample was used.

For example, suppose a census taker interviews five people in a city and discovers that the first five people he interviews are named John Smith. If he then concludes that everyone in the city must be named John Smith, then his generalization is too hasty.

Try to impress upon the audience the foolhardiness of any generalization by thinking of an example which they will recognize as too hasty. For example, if your opponent is trying to characterize Orientals as not being ready for democracy, you might point out to an audience which is sympathetic to the plight of Black people that the same sort of argument was used by Southern racists for not granting Blacks the right to vote. Southerners were a bit too hasty; maybe your opponent is too.

Composition.

The fallacy of composition is another instance of an error of arguing from individual cases to a general case or to a whole. If I examine individual baboons and find that each one separately is cowardly, may I conclude that a pack of baboons will also be cowardly? The answer is No. When in a group, baboons become extremely aggressive. This principle is used by military men who know that the properties of parts (individual soldiers) are not necessarily the properties of the whole (an army). It also finds application among rabble rousers and organizers of demonstrations. People who are otherwise rational become overly emotional and irrational when formed into a group. Or should I say mob?

The difference between composition and hasty generalization is that in hasty generalization I am making a prediction about the next individual I come across based upon the examination of other individuals of the same kind. Thus to infer that the next crow I see will be black on the basis of crows I have seen in the past might be a hasty generalization. In composition I am talking about a whole and its parts. If I have individually great architects design individually beautiful buildings, does this mean that a whole city composed of individually beautiful buildings is also beautiful? Not necessarily, because the architecture of the individual buildings may clash. It is also conceivable that a mishmash of ugliness may on sum turn out to be very exciting.

You may accuse your opponent of the fallacy of composition whenever he implies that a whole has (or does not have) a property because the parts have (or do not have) it. For example, your opponent may argue that an organization is undemocratic because the executive committee is appointed by different groups rather than elected. On the other hand, he fails to mention that decisions of the executive committee are by majority vote. The executive committee is democratic. It is not necessary that every part of an organization be democratic in order for the whole organization to be considered democratic.

Division.

Now we are concerned with arguments that move from a general principle to a particular case. One may, of course, have already attacked the general principle. On the other hand, one may accept the general principle but argue that it is not sufficient to establish the conclusion your opponent wishes to draw from it.

The fallacy of division is the fallacy of believing that a property of a whole is automatically a property of every part of the whole. For example, a work of art may be beautiful, but this in no way means that every part of that work of art is beautiful and therefore indispensable. Is the Venus de Milo not beautiful because the arms are missing? Another example is the great team which fails to have a single all-star on it. The quality of a whole, being a great team, is not necessarily a quality of every member. It works the other way as well in that individually great players may not be able to mesh and form a great team. Thus the fallacy of division is the opposite of the fallacy of composition.

Accident.

In the fallacy of accident one mistakenly applies a general principle to a specific case without realizing that the circumstances (accidents) of the individual case make the general principle inapplicable. As an example of this I am reminded of a scene from the movie *Dr. Strangelove* in which a mad general has ordered his planes to initiate an atomic war without instructions from the Pentagon. Another officer attempts to phone Washington from a pay phone in order to report the emergency but finds that he has no change. There is a vending machine nearby and the officer asks one of his men to break into it in order to obtain some change. The enlisted man refuses on the grounds that the vending machine is private property. No doubt one should not destroy private property (general principle), but in the case of preventing an atomic war (exception) the accidental circumstances invalidate the general principle.

One could argue in accusing someone of the fallacy of accident that what he is really saying is that one general principle takes precedence over another general principle. Thus he is accusing his opponent of not clearly seeing the real problem at hand. And, in general, this is what happens in an argument where two sides view the problem from different perspectives. All of this should reinforce how important it is to establish the best generalizations, in the sense of the most defensible ones, in the early part of your argument.

Another example of accident which we shall be discussing later is the argument that some people should not be punished for committing crimes (general principle) because (accidental circumstances) they are either insane or victims of their environment.

Characterizing the Conclusion.
The only test of a conclusion or principle is to extend it to the extreme in order to see how well it works. Thus whenever your opponent gives his conclusion, assume that he means it to be a general principle. For example, if he concludes that we should send aid to a country in distress (for example, Biafra), then you

should assume that he wants to send aid to every country in distress, i.e. South Vietnam, Czechoslovakia, etc. If he attempts to reject the notion that he is arguing that we should aid every country, then counter with the question why Biafrans are to be favored over other people.

The second way of directly attacking the conclusion is to criticize it for not achieving some other function or goal. For example, if you are arguing against aiding the Biafrans, then you should point out that such aid will in no way end the hostilities in the Middle East or in Southeast Asia. The specific function not achieved should be something which you think that the audience considers important.

The third way of attacking a conclusion directly is to treat your opponent's conclusion as contrary and not as contradictory. What does this mean? Usually, you and your opponent have contradictory positions, and when it becomes difficult to attack the contradictory statement you may pretend that his position is something else which you can attack more easily. Usually what you can attack more easily is the contrary statement. Let me give an example.

A. McCarthy was not a great threat.
B. McCarthy was a great threat.
C. McCarthy was no threat.

Statements A and B are contradictories. Statements B and C are contraries. A and B cannot be both true or both false at the same time. B and C can both be false at the same time but not both true.

If you are arguing B, that McCarthy was a great threat, and your opponent is arguing A, that McCarthy was not a great threat, then you should pretend that your opponent is really saying C that McCarthy was no threat. In fact, I have seen just such an argument used in a review in *The New York Times Book Review*. One man attempted to minimize, but not deny, the McCarthy threat and the reviewer simply accused him of not seeing any threat. If this kind of activity is good enough for *The New York Times,* it is certainly good enough for you.

One of the best ways of concluding a refutation of someone else's argument is to offer a *dilemma*. The structure of a dilemma will be given first, then exemplified and analyzed.

If . . . S_1 . . . , then . . . S_2 . . . ; *and*
If . . . S_3 . . . , then . . . S_4. . . .
S_1 *or* S_3.
Therefore, S_2 *or* S_4.

Consider the following example of a dilemma:

If men are good, then gun control laws are not necessary; *and* if men are bad, gun control laws will not be effective. Men are either good *or* men are bad. Therefore, gun control laws are either not necessary *or* not effective.

In the above example, S_1 corresponds to the statement "men are good." S_2 corresponds to the statement "gun control laws are not necessary." S_3 corresponds to the statement "men are bad." S_4 corresponds to the statement "gun control laws will not be effective."

The dilemma is an effective weapon because it leaves the impression that your opponent's case leads only to undesirable consequences. Since the dilemma has a standard pattern, there is no challenge in constructing it. However, it is always the case that some dilemmas are better than others. The most effective ones are built from points you have already made. Thus in the structure you should try to argue the relationship between S_1 and S_2 or the relationship between S_3 and S_4 in the earlier part of your attack. If they seem to be successful, then you may use them in the dilemma. This technique has a way of reinforcing your whole argument in the minds of the audience. Moreover, S_1 and S_3 should be a dichotomy that you think your audience will accept.

For example, in arguing against a dual legislature, the famous French Abbé Sieyès pounded away at the fact that two legislatures wasted a great deal of time duplicating each other's effort. Later he pointed out the difficulties that would follow if the two legislatures disagreed with each other. He was then able to summarize neatly his opposition in a dilemma: If the second legislature agrees with the first legislature, then the second one is superfluous; and if the second legislature disagrees with the first legislature, then the second one is pernicious. The second legislature must either agree or disagree with the first one. Therefore, the second legislature is either superfluous or pernicious.

Nonverbal Devices.

There is no reason why an attacker cannot use the same nonverbal devices as used by one who presents an argument. Therefore, you should consult the end of Chapter One for a survey of such devices. Moreover, you will have had an opportunity to survey which of these devices, if used by your opponent, was most effective and take steps to counteract it.

In addition to the foregoing devices, you should remember that a good attacker tries to choose the battlefield. That is, he tries to give the impression that his interpretation of the opposition is the only one as well as the correct one. This task will be easier if you can, as part of your attack, divert the attention of the audience from your opponent while your opponent is presenting his case. Perhaps the most famous single example of such a technique was used by the great trial lawyer Clarence Darrow. During the presentation of the prosecution's case Darrow began to smoke a very long cigar and did not flick off the ash. After a while everyone in the courtroom, including the jury, began to look at Darrow's cigar in anxious anticipation of the falling of the ash. The ash never fell, and the jury never really paid attention to the prosecution. The secret was a thin wire inserted in the center of the cigar so that the ash would be supported.

In the immediate presence of the audience, of late, I have noted some very effective nonverbal techniques of a sort. Given the proper—or should I say, improper—opponent, you may heckle either directly or indirectly by wearing an armband, carrying a sign, etc.

FACE-TO-FACE DEBATE

In addition to the techniques we have already discussed there are some special things to keep in mind if you are engaged in a face-to-face debate, cross-examinations of your opponents, or the give and take of common discussions.

There are three aims in any face-to-face debate: first, and foremost, you are trying to elicit a contradiction from your opponent; second, you are trying to embarrass the opposition publicly; third, you are trying to convince the audience of your proficiency.

Questioning.
When asking questions of your opposition your major aim is to elicit a contradiction. You do this pri-

marily by getting him to make two contradictory statements. Since he is likely to be looking out for this
possibility, it is better to *hide the conclusion* toward
which you are driving. In addition, you might ask leading questions, surreptitiously introduce the premises
you want brought out, and mix up the order so that it
is not apparent in what direction you are going. The
classic master at this sort of game is none other than
Socrates. In fact, the *Socratic method* is most easily
identified as the method of eliciting contradictions from
an opponent. A famous example of this technique is to
be found in Plato's *Republic* in a discussion of the nature of justice. The major participants in the discussion
are Socrates and Thrasymachus, who argues that justice
is whatever is in the interest of the stronger party (a
variation of the position that "might makes right").
Socrates proceeds to question Thrasymachus to see if
the position can withstand analysis.

> THRASYMACHUS: The laws are made by the ruling party
> in its own interest; a democracy makes democratic
> laws, a despot despotic ones, and so on. By making
> these laws they define as "right" for their subjects
> whatever is for their interest, and they call anyone
> who breaks these laws a wrongdoer and punish him
> accordingly. That is what I mean: in all states alike
> "right" has the same meaning, namely, what is in
> the interest of the party established in power, and
> that is the strongest. So the sound conclusion is that
> what is "right" is the same everywhere: the interest
> of the stronger party. . . .
>
> SOCRATES: No doubt you also think it is right to obey the
> men in power.
>
> THRASYMACHUS: I do.
>
> SOCRATES: Are they infallible in every type of state, or do
> they sometimes make mistakes?

THRASYMACHUS: Of course they can make a mistake.

SOCRATES: In framing laws, then, they may do their work well or badly?

THRASYMACHUS: No doubt. . . .

SOCRATES: But the subjects are to obey any law they lay down, and they will then be doing right?

THRASYMACHUS: Of course.

SOCRATES: If so by your account, it will be right to do what is not to the interest of the stronger party as well as what is.

THRASYMACHUS: What's that you're saying?

SOCRATES: Just what you said, I believe. . . . Haven't you admitted that the rulers . . . sometimes mistake their own best interests, and that at the same time it is right for the subjects to obey? . . .

THRASYMACHUS: Yes, I suppose so.

SOCRATES: Well that amounts to admitting that it is right to do what is not to the interest of the rulers or the stronger party. . . . You with your intelligence must see how that follows.

While a verbal admission of a contradiction is the most effective way of refuting an opponent, it is not always possible to obtain one. The next best thing is to point out, if possible, a contradiction or inconsistency between the spoken word and behavior. For instance, when someone attacks the capitalist system and praises what the Soviet Union is doing, you might ask him why he doesn't go live in Russia. The same sort of argument can be used with regard to Vietnam. Where would you choose to live if your choice were limited to Hanoi and Saigon?

There are of course simple cases of hypocrisy. While using the rhetoric of revolution, Norman Mailer continues to play the role of antiestablishment establishment. When asked why he did not participate in the

Chicago demonstrations during the Democratic National Convention in 1968, demonstrations which Mailer verbally supported, he replied that he did not want to be arrested because it would interfere with his presence at a series of meetings designed by his commercial publisher to publicize his latest book.

If you cannot elicit the contradiction in a formal or informal way, proceed next to try to get your opponent to become angry. Members of the audience are always ready to laugh and angering your opponent may lead him to say foolish things.

If you find that you are succeeding in your questioning and that your opponent knows this, then you may find that he refuses to accept anything you say without qualification. He may do this to stymie the progress of your line of questioning. At this point you should inject a truism like "Isn't your name . . ." or, "Isn't today's date. . . ." He must either say "yes" and you can congratulate him on being able to answer questions and then continue with your line of argument, or he can continue to say "no" and embarrass himself.

Another way of obtaining an answer you want is to ask a loaded or *complex question,* that is, a question which is so phrased that any answer given is incriminating. Actually, a complex question is really several questions in one. For example, if I ask "Are you still a member of the Communist party?" there are two possible answers. If the answer is no, then the person questioned has admitted his past membership in the Communist party. If the answer is yes, then the person has still admitted his past membership in the party. Either way, he has admitted membership. What should *he* do if he were clever and never a member of the Communist party? He should reply, instead of yes or no, simply that he has never belonged to the party.

Answering.
     Although this is a chapter on attacking someone else's case, since we have already introduced the topic of face-to-face debate, we should consider ways of answering or defending oneself in this kind of confrontation. This will lead naturally into the next chapter.

Just as the major objective of the person asking the questions is to expose a contradiction, so the major objective of the person answering the questions is to avoid a contradiction. Thus if you once discover the ultimate contradiction toward which your opponent is leading you, quickly change the subject or try to move off on a tangent and thus lead the discussion away from that issue.

If the discussion turns on some crucial matter of fact, which if answered will lead to a contradiction, then instead of denying its truth (which might prove embarrassing if you are wrong) simply declare that you are an incompetent judge on that subject and refrain from expressing an opinion. Usually it is not good form to admit ignorance, but in this case it is more important to avoid stepping into a contradiction.

One of the devices used to shake up, anger, or embarrass you will be for your opponent to declare that he does not understand what you are saying. This is usually stated in a manner indicating that you are unclear or just plain confused. Places where this device is frequently used are in the classroom where teachers use it against students and at academic gatherings where senior colleagues use it against junior colleagues. When confronted by the charge of a lack of clarity you should reply along the following lines:

"Please excuse me [ironic politeness], but with your great intellect, it should be easy to understand anything. It must be my poor statement of the issue."

Follow this by a really simple statement of the issue, that is, explain it in a patronizing manner as if the questioner were a moron. If he persists in declaring your presentation unclear, then conclude by saying, "Some people see and some people do not."

CHAPTER THREE

Defending Your Case

Among sophists there is an age-old debate about how much of a defense one should include in his initial presentation. Some feel that you should automatically defend your case by negating possible objections in the minds of the audience before they are even presented so as to leave no room for the opposition to maneuver. One objection to combining a defense along with a presentation is that the presentation tends to become obscured when lumped with a defense, a defense that inevitably includes an attack on the alternatives. Moreover, it tends to make you look defensive, as if you had something that could not stand by itself. I think that it should also be clear from a careful reading of Chapter Two that there are ways of attacking a case regardless of how it is initially presented. You cannot defuse every attacking bomb.

The purists, in addition, want to present their case unencumbered by any defense. They are proud of their ability to rebut and so welcome any and all objections, even objections by the sophisticated, because it gives them the opportunity to counterattack and object to the objectors. They can proudly point to the fact that most formal discussions allow for this sort of see-saw action. Debates usually include three parts: a presentation, a questioning period (a form of attack and defense), and an opportunity for rebuttal. The courts give both the prosecution and the defense an opportunity for an introductory statement, the presentation of a case, cross-examination, and an opportunity for a summation. There are, however, two general objections to this procedure. First, it is not always possible to get back at your opposition. The format, the audience, or the medium may only allow a single exposure. Moreover, some people lack the quickness of wit to respond rapidly in the give and take and they wish to rely more heavily upon a well thought out presentation and defense. I might add that if you are also thinking about your defense while you are preparing your presentation, you might come up with a better presentation and a better defense because you will have anticipated what the objections might be.

The moral of this debate is that you must let the circumstances determine the extent to which you combine a presentation with a defense. In any case, it is still useful to separate the different techniques of each so as to make you more self-conscious and adept at both using them and spotting them as used by others.

As is always the case when you are trying to win, the major thing to look for is audience reaction. Try to determine the extent to which your objector has been successful in breaching your defense. What particular points of yours were most easily overwhelmed, which remained steadfast and resisted all assaults, and, especially, which were ignored by the opposition? Sometimes ignoring a particular point or points is symptomatic of the opposition's inability to overcome it or the opposition's recognition that the point is so formidable it is best to call as little attention to it as possible. Your evaluation of what worked and what did not work with the audience should determine what you choose to emphasize, what you choose to ignore, and what new elements you should introduce into your defense.

There is, however, a special personal element which must be taken into account when we move to the defense, and that is your own emotional reaction to being attacked. It is one thing to be a spectator at a battle and it is quite another to be a participant. Reactions will vary with the individual, but in all cases you must learn to control your emotional responses and concentrate on winning. This suggests certain general rules for controlling yourself:

Never admit defeat:

Certainly neither look as if you have been, nor feel that you have been, defeated. If the audience detects a feeling of low morale in you, then it will immediately assume your opponent has won. There are several things you might do; for example, sit with your hands folded, avoid squirming, laugh louder than anyone else when he makes a joke, smile, take notes but not too many and take no notes at the end, or maybe pull out a copy of the *New York Review of Books* and read it, ignoring your opponent altogether if you think you can get away with it.

Refuse to be convinced:

Even if you feel that he has a good argument and that your case is weaker, refuse to be convinced of your opponent's case. This is especially important. If we give up because the opposition appears to be right we inevitably discover after it is too late that we were really right in the first place. How often have you thought of an adequate answer and rebuttal after the debate was over? Trust your initial instincts!

Retain your self-confidence:

It always hurts to have someone think ill either of you or your case, especially if your opponent has some sort of prestige. In order to build up your self-confidence and to offset the image you have of your opposition, try the following. Imagine that the man or woman or institution who has attacked you is standing there in front of you and the audience without any clothes on. This is enough to make anybody look ridiculous. Or imagine the special kind of ignorance, stupidity, blindness, or combinations thereof which might possibly lead someone to disagree with your case.

Do not underestimate the opposition:

If you do you are likely to let your guard down and cause your opposition to win by your own default. The best way to accomplish this general end and to retain your self-confidence is to think of your opposition as *evil.* It is not just the case that the opposition is wrong, but it is also dishonest and unscrupulous in intent.

A defense is also an attack:

Do not simply defend your own position but attack the opposition as well. You attack not only to show that the argument of the opposition is merely persuasive in a superficial way, but also to give yourself more time to think of a reply in defending your own case. But at all times give the impression that you are in charge of the argument.

COUNTERATTACK

Every defense must have a counterattack, that is, a refutation of the charges made against your case by the opposition. Needless to say, not every attack against your case will contain every kind of charge, so that you will have to use only some of the following techniques, depending upon what your opponent uses.

Statement of Your Case.

There is one thing you should always claim no matter what the opposition has said, namely, that the opposition has misstated your case. No matter what the opposition has said, you should make this claim because *(a)* if the opposition has misstated your case because it misunderstood your case, then by implication the opposition must not be very bright; *(b)* if the opposition has misstated your case but understands your case very well, then by implication the opposition is dishonest; *(c)* this gives you the opportunity to restate your case, and you want to restate your case so as (1) to reinforce in the minds of the audience what you want to discuss; (2) to reformulate your case in order to sidestep some of the objections made, a point we shall see in greater detail below; and finally (3) to give yourself a little more time before you reply.

All or Nothing Mistake.

Since one of the major ways in which a case is attacked is to extend it to an extreme, a point we made in Chapter Two, you must be prepared to offset this kind of tactic if it is used against you. If you did not make a generalization or categorical statement and your opponent accuses you of having done so, then reiterate the more modest case which you were presenting. In addition imply that your opponent is so intent upon seeing every issue as clearly black and white that he misses all of the subtleties and nuances of your argument. For example, in arguing for the use of methadone, a heroin substitute, you admit all of the shortcomings of the methadone program, especially the fact that it too is addictive. But you reiterate that it is a temporary program that is superior to any other program which has been tried. It is not a panacea, but it does do some good. Moreover, reiterate that you are not opposed to other programs.

As another example, suppose you argue that nationalism or national pride was a major if not the major factor in the colonization of Africa and Asia by Western European countries during the nineteenth and early twentieth centuries. Your opponent might counter with the standard Marxist-Leninist thesis by pointing out the economic advantages which colonial powers expected or obtained. Not only are there exceptions to your opponent's case (you show he is wrong), but you do not have to deny his point in order to substantiate your own. It may very well be true that economic gain was one factor in colonization, but this does not show that nationalism was not also a factor. In fact you can still argue that nationalism was more important as a factor than economics.

Appeal to Ignorance.

The inability to disprove your case is tantamount to a proof that it is correct. As long as nobody can show that you are absolutely mistaken, then act as if you are absolutely right. Keep harping upon the fact that some of the things you said, even if they are trivial, are right and that the opposition cannot disprove your case.

There are two good examples of this. First, how

would someone go about disproving the existence of God? I do not see how, in the case of something like God, one can. Does this prove that God exists?

Second, no conspiracy theory can be disproved. How would one go about showing that all of the conspiracy explanations of how President John F. Kennedy was killed are incorrect? As long as the conspiracy theories are *compatible* with the known evidence, no disproof is possible. Of course compatibility is not the same thing as proof for the simple reason that an infinite number of compatible possibilities can be invented. Nevertheless, there is in the popular mind the irresistible temptation to take compatibility for proof.

Statistics.

If you used statistics, and if your opponent attacked your use of statistics in the manner we indicated in Chapter Two, then your defense should be as follows. On the one hand, if he accuses you of not using a random, representative, or adequate sample, you counter this by asking him to *define what a random sample is.* He will be unable to define a random sample because no one, not even the most sophisticated statistical analyst, has been able to define a random sample. The reason for this is interesting and worth dwelling upon.

Statistical information consists of a mathematically expressed relationship between two or more things. For example, the number of smallpox cases decreases in an area or within a group when those people are inoculated. Perhaps there is an 88 percent decrease in the number of cases. However, no amount of statistical information can establish an invariable or causal relationship between two or more things without independent evidence. The whole point of using statistical evidence is that it is only used *when we do not know the direct connection* or complex of connections among things.

For example, in studying crime statistics we may note a high correlation between crime and membership in certain ethnic groups. What does this tell us? That members of certain groups are more criminally prone? That there is a police conspiracy to arrest or pursue more vigorously members of certain ethnic groups? That there is a hidden cause or causes (another factor) which might lead members of a certain ethnic group to commit more crime? One may use statistical evidence to discover a problem (you notice high correlations which may or may not mean anything) or to back up some theory about why certain things happen. But without the theory, the evidence makes no sense. Hence statistical evidence by itself does not prove or disprove anything, but together with other pieces of information it may be meaningful. Anyone who attacks your statistical evidence and ignores the rest of your case can have this truth pointed out to him and to the audience.

On the other hand, if your opponent attacks the use of statistics in general, you may provide a counter-example to show how silly that would be. Suppose there were a dread disease which did not exist among a certain portion of the population because they ate a certain food. In other words a high statistical correlation exists between a food and the absence of a disease. Wouldn't you eat that food even though the direct connection is unknown to you?

As for the charge that you either neglected or suppressed certain facts, you may make the same counter-charge by introducing some facts that you had not mentioned before and turning the question on your adversary. Why didn't he mention that information? This, by the way, reinforces an earlier point we made about saving some ammunition for later instead of using everything in your initial presentation.

Defense of Generalizations. Your generalizations are attacked when someone tries to point out that there is an exception to them. There are three answers to this charge.

First, the exception may be irrelevant to the point you are trying to make. Suppose you are talking about mammals and the fact that females have milk-producing mammae. Your opponent may note that some mammals are not born alive but as eggs, as in the case of the duck-billed platypus. This is true but irrelevant.

Second, you may claim that the exception is not really an exception and accuse your opponent of *special pleading*. You argue that the grounds on which he claims to make an exception (attacks based on the charges of accident or division) are not good grounds. For example, during the 1970 trial of Black Panther leader Bobby Seale, William Sloan Coffin, chaplain at Yale University, argued that Seale should not be tried, convicted, and punished even if he were guilty because society had been responsible for making him a criminal. This is an exception by genetic explanation. You might argue that this is special pleading. Would Coffin want to release a Southern racist who led a lynch mob on the grounds that society (in the form of Reconstruction) had caused this man to become a kind of criminal? To argue for the genetic explanation in one case and not in the other is to be guilty of special pleading.

The third defense against the charge of a hasty generalization (or the existence of an exception to your generalization) is to fall back on the wise saying that "the exception proves the rule" and hope for the best. This, by the way, implies (but do not tell anyone about it) that the more exceptions there are the better is the rule. That does sound strange! Actually, the original statement was made by Francis Bacon and when he said it the word "prove" meant "test." You test a generalization by looking for exceptions. Rather than helping the generalization, the exception invalidates it.

In Defense of Definitions.

Definitions can be challenged as being either too strict or too permissive in the sense of being unusual. If you are charged with taking terms too narrowly, and especially if you are charged with making your position true by definition, then reply that we must have clear thoughts, otherwise equivocation will be the undoing of us all. Enter into a tirade about how your opponent is a sloppy thinker who objects to those who strive for clarity.

Suppose you are charged with misusing a word, misusing it in the sense that your use is not recognized by the dictionary. What do you do? Here you enter into a tirade against dictionaries. By whom and how are dictionaries put together? What makes these men qualified to decide?

The question is, are dictionaries descriptive or normative? That is, do they describe actual usage or do they prescribe how we ought to use a term? If they are descriptive, then the dictionary is obviously incorrect because it does not describe how you use the term. If it is replied that dictionaries describe general usage and not peculiar usage, then cast doubt on this. Have you ever been polled by a dictionary maker on how you use a term? Has there ever been a national referendum on usage?

Now try the other approach. Suppose dictionaries are prescriptive, that is, they tell us how we ought to use a word. Who are the dictionary makers to decide such crucial issues in life anyway? Are they people who already hold views opposed to yours? If so, then it is the dictionary makers who are trying to win arguments by making certain views true by definition. Moreover, if this keeps up we shall end up with what Orwell described in *1984* as Newspeak, a language constantly manipulated for the benefit of a few.

Quoting Out of Context.

Like any other charge, this one should be denied and continually denied. Keep insisting that the words you quoted are exactly as you said they were, that is, you ignore the charge that you quoted out of context and pretend that you were charged with misquoting.

If your opponent pursues this point or you are forced to engage in a prolonged discussion of it, then raise the broader issue of what constitutes the proper context. Is it the phrase, sentence, or sentences you quoted, or is it something larger? Accuse your opponent of being ornery: If I quote the sentence, then he will say I did not quote the whole paragraph, and if I quote the whole paragraph then he will say that I deliberately ignored the preceding or following paragraphs, until finally I shall have to end up quoting everything written in the English language—or is that too small a context?

If you are really trapped by a skillful adversary who finds some way of convincing the audience that you have used an improper or misleading linguistic context, then claim that the proper context includes the gestures and behavior of the person you quoted. Since there is no generally agreed upon context in terms of which we interpret gestures and behavior, who can really accuse one of misreading someone else's position?

Legal minds, particularly those of scholars of the U.S. Constitution, have a flair for this kind of interpretation. Some of them are said to be 'loose constructionists' of the Constitution, and others are said to be 'strict constructionists.' Much is made of this distinction, but actually there is little to be said for it. If anyone were really strict he could never extend or apply the Constitution to a single case. Every reading involves an interpretation. When we speak of the spirit of the law we are advocating a much freer interpretation. But what exactly did the framers of the Constitution mean by some of the things they said? For an understanding of this, we have to consult some of their other writings, and this is exactly what is done. But which other writings? What is the proper context? This is a real problem even when we are not trying to be devious.

Inconsistency.

If you are accused of being inconsistent, deny it! Deny it! First, there may be a simple misunderstanding involved and you can easily clear it up. Second, there may be no problem at all and the accusation is merely an attempt on the part of the opposition to embarrass you. In this case, you should point it out and publicly chastise the opposition. Third, there may very well be an inconsistency which you overlooked. In this case, you should confidently move to reinterpret what you said so as to make the contradiction disappear.

For example, suppose you are advocating social

reform for an oppressed group of people and you publicly argue that the oppressed must take the law into their own hands, they must use violence to get justice; you then pull out a machete and wave it while you quote Patrick Henry's famous statement, "Give me liberty or give me death!" Later, when you are arrested and tried for inciting to riot, sedition, etc., you claim that you made no such inflammatory remarks because your words were not to be taken literally, they were only political rhetoric. What you had really meant was that people should only do this if necessary or forced to but actually at this time you really believe that conditions will allow for more moderate means of social reform.

Depending upon the situation and the audience, there may be times when inconsistency is not a bad thing. After all, is not a foolish consistency the hobgoblin of little minds? Didn't the famous German philosopher Hegel deny the law of the excluded middle which is the logical foundation of inconsistency? All right, then, I am inconsistent. So what of it?

This technique is especially useful when you invoke a higher truth than the limited ones to which the laws of inconsistency apply. For example, Herbert Marcuse, grandfather of the New Left, claims that the news media distort in their reports of the news. He wants the real truth. Next he claims that they report the death of civil rights workers in the same tone of voice as they report the weather. What he wants is a more emotional report. Wouldn't this be a form of bias? Isn't Marcuse being inconsistent? No. He appeals to a higher truth which he claims is more than science. In addition, Marcuse is an expert on Hegel.

Red Herring.

So far we have been discussing refutations of specific charges made against your presentation. If you have successfully rebutted them, all well and good. But what happens if you feel that your defense has not been strong enough or that there are lingering doubts in the minds of the audience? At this point you should avoid sticking to the point. Remember that the only thing that always sticks to the point is a dead insect on display. What you must do is draw attention to a side issue where you feel particularly strong. This will give the impression that you are still in charge of the course of the discussion.

There are several things to keep in mind when casting out a red herring. First, although it is a side issue, it must be related at least indirectly to the issue you are discussing or the audience will not accept it. You cannot introduce as a red herring the question about the price of eggs when discussing astronomy. Second, the issue you introduce must have sufficient emotional appeal to catch attention immediately. It should be so strong that you can work it as long as you want. Third, you must make sure that you present this issue in such a way that you and the audience inevitably end up on the same side while your opponent ends up on the other side.

A particularly interesting version of the red herring is to be found in the discussions concerning cures for social ills. Imagine a debate about improving the education of ghetto children wherein Side One claims that some proposal (let us call it X) is the way to solve the problem. Let us suppose further that Side Two attacks X on the grounds that it is inherently self-contradictory, has failed when used before, will interfere with other programs, and costs too much anyway. Side One, in defense of its proposal which has now been ripped to shreds, introduces the following red herring: you do not really understand and sympathize with the problem. Side One then proceeds to elaborate a lengthy presentation of the problem: the horror of the ghetto, the warped lives of the children, the lack of a future, and their eventual destruction. By the end of this red herring, the audience is in tears. If the audience does not think that Side Two is racist, it certainly thinks Side Two is insensitive. Moreover, the audience will not only approve of proposal X, they would probably approve of any proposal.

Why is this a red herring? The argument was about a specific proposal X to solve a particular problem. At no time was the problem itself under discussion. Side Two never denied the existence of the problem, they only attacked proposal X as a way of solving the problem. Side One, which defended proposal X, never really answered the criticism about their proposal, instead they acted as if Side Two was denying the existence of the problem. The red herring was related (at least in content), it was highly emotional, and Side One took the side it believed would be shared by the audience.

Call for Perfection.

One possibility should never be forgotten: your case or proposal may be a good one but it may not be perfect. That is, there may be problems or objections to it which cannot be satisfactorily answered. This, however, does not imply that your solution is not the best available. There are times when it is necessary to admit that there are objections but they do not invalidate your proposal. Here you accuse your opposition of wanting perfection or Utopia before they will accept any proposal.

This kind of problem, objection, and defense figured very prominently during the debate over civil rights legislation. Civil rights advocates had introduced legislation designed to protect Blacks against race prejudice and harassment. The opponents to civil rights legislation (including presidential candidate Goldwater) argued that the only way the race prejudice problem would be solved (really) was when some men experienced a change of heart. Legislation would not do the trick. In answer to this objection, civil rights advocates (including Martin Luther King, Jr.) pointed out that they did not have time to wait for a perfect mankind. In the meantime the laws would at least change behavior, and that was some kind of progress even if it was not Utopia.

As a supplement to this kind of defense you can argue that your proposal will, or might eventually, lead to removing all difficulties. As Dr. King pointed out, the change in men's behavior created by the laws might eventually lead to changes in their hearts.

Nothing-but Objections.

A variation of the call for perfection is the simple articulation of objections. The problem is not whether my proposal is perfect, but whether it would be better to do nothing or even whether there is an alternative.

There are two versions of the defense against nothing-but objections. We might call version one the "less sincere" version. Here we argue that even though our proposal is not perfect we should all adopt it anyway because no one can think of a better one. I offer the three following examples of the less sincere version.

(1) Cure for cancer: periodic human sacrifice to the sun god; (2) Cure for war: drinking milk shakes; (3) Removal of warts: drinking Irish whisky. No doubt there are people who will not like my suggested solutions, but can they offer an alternative which will prove to be more immediately successful?

The second version should be called the "more sincere" version. There, as is so often the case in life's great moral dilemmas, we must choose between two evils and hope that we choose the lesser. It is very important in cases like this that they involve two clear and evil courses of action with no other alternatives. Imagine you are trapped in a tower with a mentally deranged man who (1) does not know you are present, and (2) is shooting at and killing people passing below. Every second you hesitate to do something he kills another person; he is too strong for you to overpower; there is no prospect of immediate help either from the outside or from God; the only way you can stop him is to kill him from behind with the small hand gun you have. Should you kill him? No doubt this is not a pleasant decision and you will be destroying life. On the other hand, what is the alternative? Can you seriously hesitate because someone else might later object to the taking of life?

Damning the Dilemma.

There are three ways of handling a dilemma, but before we discuss them let us remind ourselves what a dilemma is. A dilemma supposedly offers you two alternatively undesirable consequences. It is an argument having two premises and a conclusion:

If . . . S_1 . . . then S_2 . . ; *and* if . . . S_3 . . . then S_4.
S_1 *or* S_3.

Therefore, S_2 *or* S_4.

The following is an example of a dilemma:

If the police are given a free hand, then they will interfere with our civil liberties; *and* if the police are not given a free hand, then they will not be able to prevent crime. Either the police are given a free hand *or* they are not given a free hand. *Therefore,* the police must either interfere with our civil liberties *or* the police will not be able to suppress or prevent crime.

The first way of answering a dilemma is to *grasp one or the other horn*. We do this by rejecting the truth of one or the other conditional statements (a conditional statement is a statement of the if . . . then form). In our example we have two conditionals: if the police are given a free hand, then they will interfere with our civil liberties; *and* if the police are not given a free hand, then they will not be able to prevent crime.

We might easily reject the latter conditional by pointing out that the police do not at present have a free hand and they certainly do prevent some crime, even if not all crime.

The second way of refuting a dilemma is to *go between the horns,* that is, to reject the second premise as not providing mutually exclusive alternatives. Our second premise was: either the police are given a free hand, *or* they are not given a free hand. The second half of the premise assumes that the police are completely restricted in what they do. However, there is a third alternative. We can place some restrictions on police behavior (eliminate the third degree, *habeas corpus,* etc.) but we give them some discretionary powers. This is in fact what we do.

The third way of refuting a dilemma is the most beautiful. Just as a dilemma was a very effective rhetorical device to end a series of objections, so a *counter-dilemma* is a beautiful and effective way of dismissing the whole case of the opposition. First look at the structure of a dilemma above and then note how a simple change below provides a foolproof formula for constructing a counterdilemma:

If . . . S_1 . . . then . . . not $= S_4$; *and* if . . . S_3 . . . then . . . not $= S_2$.

S_1 *or* S_3.

Therefore, not $= S_4$ *or* not $= S_2$.

In other words, what we have done is to reverse the order of S_2 and S_4 and negated them. What does the counterdilemma look like?

If the police are given a free hand then they will prevent all crime (double negative here: original statement said not-prevent, here not-not-prevent is equivalent to prevent); and if they are not given a free hand, then they will *not* interfere with our civil liberties.

Either the police are given a free hand or they are not given a free hand. (Second premise remains the same.)

Therefore, the police must either prevent all crime *or* the police will not interfere with our civil liberties.

As you can see, the counterdilemma gives two equally attractive alternatives with the same information supplied by the original dilemma. It is effective against an opponent not because it really says anything, but because it shows how much more clever you are than he.

No discussion of dilemmas and counterdilemmas would be complete without including the famous example of the logic teacher and his pupil. The logic teacher advertised that any one of his students who lost his first court case would not have to pay the fee. Soon one of the students who completed the course announced outright that he refused to pay for the course of instruction. The logic teacher sued, taking the student to court.

In his defense the student argued: If I lose this case, then I do not have to pay the teacher (by advertisement); and if I win then I do not have to pay (by court decision). Either I win or I lose. Therefore, either I do not have to pay, or I do not have to pay. Either way I do not have to pay.

The teacher argued on his own behalf: If you win this case, then you must pay me (by advertisement); if you lose this case, then you must pay me (by court decision). Either you win this case or you lose this case. Therefore, either you pay me or you pay me. Either way you have to pay me.

Appeal to Self-interest.

Just as in your presentation you pointed out some residual benefits of accepting your point of view, so in the defense of your presentation against your opponent's attacks you may repeat the appeal. However, here there should be a difference. In the presentation you appealed to some general interest shared by the whole, but here your appeal should be the very narrow self-interest of the immediate audience. For example, in a debate about the value of the United Nations let us suppose you present a list of all the values and accomplishments and promise of the world forum. Your opponent denigrates its actual accomplishments and even points out how much harm such an organization may do (e.g., easy access of spies to America). In your defense you will, of course, answer all of the objections worth answering. But there is no reason why you cannot add an appeal to narrow self-interest. When speaking to a New York City audience you might as well point out how much money the United Nations contributes to the economy of the city. However, be wary of an opponent who appeals to self-interest by pointing out the city's expenses due to the United Nations, i.e., police protection.

The first stage of a successful defense is the repulsion of specific charges and assaults on your initial presentation. The second stage of defense is an attack on the alternatives. This is especially important if the first stage of your defense has not been as successful as you would have liked. Most arguments are won by showing that one side is better on balance, that is, has more assets and fewer liabilities.

However, if your original or first-stage defense has been successful, or if during the second stage of your defense you become successful, then an attack on the alternative position becomes a way of annihilating the enemy and winning the argument. In short, not only is your position defensible but theirs is not.

Damning the Alternative.
Naturally enough, the first procedure in the move to win is called damning the alternative. There are three possibilities here: (a) if your opponent explicitly offers an alternative, attack it: (b) if your opponent only has an implicit position, bring his case out into the open and attack it; and (c) if he fails to offer any kind of alternative, then argue that there is no acceptable alternative

to your position because if there were one then your opponent would have offered it. Thus you win by default.

As an example, we may take your defense of an "open society" (in the social, political, and economic sense). No doubt there are many shortcomings of an open society, but you can doubtlessly defend some of these as being either not really shortcomings or as necessary evils. For instance, in an open society there is competition and a great deal of wasteful controversy. However, this is a small price to pay for the great release of creative energy which this makes possible. But, in addition to your defense of an open society, you can honestly ask: what is the alternative? Aren't the so-called advantages of a totalitarian society illusory if not repressive? No defense of an open society has to deny its shortcomings; it has only to ask, is there a viable alternative?

Two Wrongs Make a Right.

Any shortcoming of your position that cannot be defended can still be justified by pointing out the errors or shortcomings of the opposition. The difference between this technique and the one described above is the following. In the case of damning the alternative, you are claiming that on balance your position is better. In the case of "two wrongs make a right" you are claiming that certain apparent liabilities are really justified or caused by the errors of the opposition.

For example, let us imagine two countries at war. Country A has as its stated policy that torture is necessary and that the mass murder of civilians is necessary. In other words, atrocities are justified. Country B is opposed to atrocities. It does not excuse atrocities and when its soldiers commit them they are punished.

Therefore, Country B is less likely to have atrocities committed by its personnel. This is a damning of the alternative.

On the other hand, when both countries resort to atrocities as a matter of policy, and not inadvertently on the part of some undisciplined soldiers, then we are not damning the alternative. When Country B says that its atrocities are justified because Country A resorts to atrocities, then the technique of "two wrongs make a right" is being used.

Another example of this is the suppression of the rights of free speech of some people on the grounds that those people themselves advocate censorship. For example, Communists do not advocate free speech in their views of what society should be. To deny them the rights of free speech in our society because they would deny free speech to us is to argue that two wrongs make a right.

For those who are enamored of the principle that two wrongs make a right, may I suggest the following consideration. Imagine how glorious and sublime three wrongs would be!

Ad hominem.

This most useful technique seems to appear everywhere. Instead of attacking the specific points of an argument, you attack the man. The special version to be used here is a way of making the audience believe that you have already successfully repulsed every part of your opponent's attack and now it is time to finish him off. This is like a postwar trial for the losers wherein you document the evil ways of the opponent. You tell your audience how someone falls into the trap of believing such nonsense.

As examples, we all know that believers in the establishment are that way because they have been seduced by their vested interests; we all know that revolutionaries are simply the alienated sick of a society.

Appeal to Ignorance.
In this version we argue that because the opposition cannot prove its case, our case must be true by default.

For example, the Warren Commission report has not convinced everyone because there are a few loose ends in its evaluation of the evidence. The failure of the Warren Commission report to convince everyone beyond a shadow of a doubt automatically (so this technique would claim) means that those who have argued for a group conspiracy are right. One of the major assumptions behind this technique is that the alternatives discussed are the only possible alternatives.

This technique is especially useful against any new idea or suggestion to adopt some policy that has never been tried before. If an idea has never been tried before, then obviously no one really knows if it is or will be a good one. Therefore, since we cannot prove it is good, it must be bad. Thus a proposal to make abortions legal may be opposed on the grounds that no one really knows for sure whether it will achieve its desired ends. As you can see, this version of the appeal to ignorance will be very useful to killjoys and conservatives.

Certain legal systems rely heavily upon it. In the Anglo-Saxon system a man is innocent until proven guilty and he need not incriminate himself. In Continental systems a man is guilty until he proves that he is innocent. This is clearly an appeal to ignorance of the second type. By the way, how do you prove that you are innocent?

Invincible Ignorance and Falsification.

In this form of attack on your opposition you accuse your opponent of clinging to principles or beliefs which he *(a)* accepts uncritically, *(b)* refuses to debate, and *(c)* offers no criteria for refutation or falsifiability.

There are people, for example, who believe in the Communist conspiracy, in the conspiracy of the military-industrial complex, or in the unbridgeable gap between business and labor, and they believe these things as matters of almost religious conviction. It is thus not the specific belief but the manner in which it is held that makes it subject to the charge of invincible ignorance. They refuse to listen to any criticism of their beliefs, they will not debate or discuss the matter, and most important of all they will not specify what would count against their belief.

The last criterion, falsifiability, is a critical one. It is almost a definition of rationality to say that a man is rational to the extent that he will tell you under what circumstances he will change his mind. To know when a belief will be considered false is to know how to reason with someone who holds that belief. It is a mark of psychosis that someone will not under any circumstances change his mind. To expose your opponent as one who holds this kind of belief is to undermine the audience's tolerance of him as a rational man.

Most people could, of course, if given enough time and help, specify when they would consider their beliefs disconfirmed. However, most people never really think about this point. You should take advantage of this lapse in attention and charge your opponent with invincible ignorance frequently. You will be surprised how often it will work.

Appeal to Force or Fear (Ad baculum).

There is no more effective technique for assuring your audience how much better your position is than your opponent's than pointing out the dire consequences which will follow the adoption of his proposal. Here you are appealing to fear.

An example of the appeal to fear is the claim or prediction made by insurance salesmen about the death of the father and eventual suffering of the family. If all else fails, this fearful consequence will close the deal. What responsible father wants to think of his wife and children suffering after he has gone? After all, didn't this happen to so-and-so who lived around the corner, etc. In case the father is really hardhearted, the salesman, if he is any good, will elaborate this argument at length to the wife. Here a little forceful persuasion is in order.

In arguments involving human behavior, one interesting element introduced into predictions of dire consequences is the possible threat of a self-fulfilling prophecy. Here you not only predict the dire consequence, but intimate in the most tactful way that you might even bring such a dire consequence about if your position is not adopted. For example, how often have you heard a spokesman for the Blacks say, "If you do not improve the lot of the Blacks and meet their demands there will be riots." How often have you heard the opponents of such demands say, "If you surrender to Black extremist demands there will be a white backlash." Both of these statements are not just predictions but subtle threats.

Abandon Discussion.

If you are absolutely convinced that you have overwhelmed your opponent, then you should cut off debate as soon as possible. To pursue the discussion beyond the point at which you have clearly won is to give your opponent an opportunity he does not deserve, it is to risk throwing away your victory, and it is to lend credibility to your opponent's case. Once you have won, cut off the discussion by saying something like, "I never argue with a man who is wrong!"

Going for a Tie

Nobody wins them all. Not only will you have bad days but the opposition may just be lucky or the audience a bunch of complete dimwits. Hence you cannot expect to win them all. Suppose you have counter-attacked as much as you could, and suppose you have tried to win but you simply cannot achieve a decisive and clear-cut victory, then what do you do? You go for a tie!

Do not admit defeat:

Under no circumstances should you admit defeat. Remember that there are three possible stages of your position: *(a)* you are completely right; or *(b)* you are mostly right but your position needs a few qualifications and correction; or *(c)* you knowingly defended a weak position in order to dramatically call attention to a useful underlying principle.

True by definition:

You can always save your position by making it true by definition. This is not a victory. When you are forced to use this technique as a form of defense it always leaves the audience with the impression that your position was trivial and the argument almost a waste of time. But still this is better than losing. Suppose, for example, you have argued that abortion is always an act of murder. No matter what your opposition throws at you, you will always be right if you say you mean by murder the destruction of any living cell. The implications of this position might be pretty silly, e.g., destruction of plant life is murder, but you will at least be safe in your claim that abortion is murder.

Forestalling disagreement:
Perhaps a more effective technique when you must go for a tie is to argue that your opponent really agrees with your position. Thus there is no real argument and no real disagreement. This tactic is so surprising to some people that when, after having demolished their opponent, they find him claiming that everybody agrees, they fall right into the trap of being nice. Usually people who are interested in the truth fall into it.

The man who was most successful in using this technique was Paul Tillich, the famous theologian. He offered proofs of God's existence and arguments for a new view of religion. When attacked, and sometimes he was severely criticized and effectively refuted, he would fall back on the technique of arguing that the opponent really agreed. Even the opponent's respect for logic was in Tillich's view a sign of ultimate concern and therefore a proof of God's existence.

It is difficult to argue against this technique. The only way out is to keep insisting upon the differences in the positions. The risk you run when you try to wiggle out of someone else's use of forestalling disagreement is that you might alienate the audience. After all, he is trying to be nice and you are being a bastard. Here what you must do is restate the case of the one who is trying to forestall disagreement, restate it in such a manner that you appear the victor and welcome his repentance. For example, as long as Tillich draws no moral or social implications from his position, as long as he admits his differences with traditional theology, and as long as he etc., etc., then I welcome his conversion.

Invitation:

When you see that you cannot do anything else, give a summary of the progress of the argument, including the positions of both sides. Make this summary as positive and as friendly as possible. Organize it so that it looks as progressive as possible, that is, as if the argument has been heading progressively in a certain direction almost by prearrangement. Conclude with the remark that we have not come to the end or final determination, and *issue an invitation to your opponent to join you in the common search for the truth.*

CHAPTER FOUR

Political Propaganda

The expression "political propaganda" sounds almost redundant to us because we usually take propaganda to mean political propaganda. However, the term "propaganda" did not always have that meaning. Originally, the term "propaganda" referred to a committee of cardinals of the Roman Catholic church whose primary responsibility was to direct the foreign missions. Needless to add, among their functions was to convert foreigners to their faith. Gradually the word propaganda took on the meaning of trying to convert others to one's belief, usually a political belief. In more recent times, the word has taken on a new wrinkle, in that propaganda is not only directed outwardly to potential converts, but there is even a form of propaganda for reinforcing the belief of the faithful. Usually we call this kind of propaganda "improving morale."

Perhaps the most efficient modern student of political propaganda was Adolf Hitler. In *Mein Kampf* his point of departure for the discussion of propaganda was to compare it to commercial advertising. Like advertising, propaganda is usually directed to the masses, most of whom have a very limited intelligence or make very limited use of their intelligence. Hence if it is to be effective, propaganda must (1) be limited to a few issues; (2) use these issues like slogans; and (3) avoid cleverness and dilution.

The direction of all effective propaganda must be the exclusive emphasis on the position you are trying to sell. Hence there should be no consideration of the assets of alternative position, nor should there be any implication that the opposition has anything to offer. "Propaganda's task is . . . not to evaluate the various rights, but . . . to stress exclusively the one that is to be represented by it."

If propaganda is to represent everything as black or white, then what is one to do with the opposition's position? Here propaganda combines presentation and defense: anticipate the objections of the opposition and present your position in such a way that, without having to mention them, all of the objections are answered. In fact, it is because political propaganda must be so exclusive that it is a peculiar mixture of presentation, attack, and defense all rolled into one.

In terms of the devices it uses, both verbal and nonverbal, political propaganda is very interesting. Although everyone has great respect for the written word, I doubt that written tracts are very effective. If anything, the shorter the presentation the better. Hence the political tract is replaced by the mimeographed leaflet and this in turn eventually gives way to the political poster. The poster may be relatively sophisticated, as in a cartoon, conveying either a sense of horror (moral outrage) or humor directed against the opposition. But the ultimate in brevity of force is the slogan.

Before discussing specific slogans there is one other piece of advice that will help us to understand political slogans. "It belongs to a great leader's genius that he contrives always to make opponents of quite different kinds look as if they belonged to the same category." Hitler himself did this rather effectively, condemning his archenemies Marxists and Jews at the same time by noting that Marx had a Jewish upbringing.

One of the great political slogans of our time is the concept of a "Communist conspiracy" which is invoked indiscriminately by some Congressional leaders to condemn a wide assortment of real and imagined enemies. The conspiracy covers some of the following: Russian attempts at hegemony, Communist Chinese nationalism, some diverse forms of African nationalism, and all movements in the United States, regardless of differences, which are directed to improving the lot of the Blacks and other ethnic groups.

In the 1964 presidential campaign, the Democrats overwhelmed Goldwater by some simple devices such as showing a brief film of a child playing and then the explosion of an atomic bomb. The slogan that reduced Goldwater to a militarist was very effective.

In the current Vietnam War debate, the so-called peace movement, symbolized by ☮, lumps all of its opposition into one group and by calling itself the peace movement implies that the opposition is against peace. This is extremely clever because offhand I cannot think of anyone who is against peace. The peace symbol represents a more or less vague view on how peace is to be achieved rather than the position that it should be achieved. Everyone is for the same end, although not necessarily by the same means. On the other side, the American flag has been appropriated by right-wing groups who fail to distinguish between patriotism and their particular political views.

When propaganda is directed toward members one considers as part of the faithful, or as strongly leaning toward the faithful, some interesting devices are used. To reinforce agreement among a current constituency, you make strong emotional appeals to previously agreed upon ideals and symbols. Thus in seeking support for the administration's foreign policy, the spokesmen will appeal to the flag, loyalty, and support of our troops overseas. To reinforce unity among constituents you exaggerate differences from the opposition. Thus even though college students differ sharply among themselves on foreign policy issues, those who speak for the peace movement will take one of Nixon's remarks directed against a specific group called "bums" and claim that Nixon is insulting the whole college community, which he is not. They reply "we are all bums," thereby exaggerating the differences between Nixon and some college students and playing down differences among the students themselves.

Before going into a more detailed analysis of political rhetoric, we should point out how effective the spoken word is as opposed to the written word or even to the use of television. This will help to explain why technology will not make any appreciable difference in political campaigning. Using the spoken word is superior because you can gauge audience reaction continually. Hitler even speculated that people are more receptive to speeches in the evening. In giving a political speech, one looks for three things:

(1) Have you aroused the interest of the audience?
(2) Does the audience understand what you are saying?
(3) Are they convinced?

In the analysis of a political position, you will discover the appeal to pity in the depiction of the plight of those victimized by the opposition. One also finds appeals *ad populum* in the waving of the flag; appeals to precedent, as in discussions of the "legality" of the Vietnam War; and the ever present experts or authorities on foreign policy such as John Wayne, Leonard Bernstein, and the endless petitions of academics in *The New York Times*. One is constantly assaulted by statistics: the war dead compared to "similar" situations, i.e., the Spanish-American War; the number of tons of rice captured, etc. We are offered analogies to Munich and the appeasement, or perhaps analogies with Nazi aggression (Joan Baez compares the U.S. to the SS).

There are many political examples in the first three chapters which you can review if you want to see them in context. What I am concerned with here is the special kinds or forms of argument used in political debates, and especially the most recurrent forms.

Red herring:

In combating an opponent in political debate one must constantly reiterate what has not been denied or continually ignore what has actually been asserted. You do not answer your opponent, you simply hit him with a red herring. For instance, Vice President Agnew has sharply attacked the press and news media many times for what he considers to be its unfair coverage of political events. In reply to this attack, which should have been either an explicit denial or an admission of guilt and the promise of repentance, the news media responded by charging Agnew with the attempt to impose censorship. They were effective in that many people have requested Agnew to moderate his attacks. There was nothing in Agnew's speech that implied censorship.

The media responded emotionally to the censorship threat, real or imagined, and forgot the main issue raised, the media's one-sided presentation of political events.

Between heaven and hell:
The most incredible and incongruous combinations of appeals to ideals and appeals to self-interest are combined in political rhetoric. As an instance, I shall quote from a letter that appeared in *The New York Times* signed by several prominent senators, including Senator McGovern:

> We are joining in this statement to make plain our deep conviction that our vital national interests are, indeed, involved in preserving the balance of power in the Middle East pending a final settlement of the Arab-Israeli dispute.
>
> There are fundamental differences between the the situation in Indo-China and the situation in Israel.
>
> The government of Israel is a democracy. This is not true of the regimes our armed forces are supporting in Southeast Asia. Israel asks only that we sell her the military equipment....
>
> South Vietnam ... asks that we give them—not sell them —the military equipment to defend their own forms of repression against other forms of repression. Worse yet, they ask that we spill American blood and spend American lives in their behalf. Israel makes no such demands on us....

We are not here discussing the merits of the two respective cases, nor are we even quarreling with the conclusion. The question to ask here is the following: Should an interest which is vital to America be defended with money, blood, and lives? If the Middle-East balance of power is vital to our national interests, then it should be an area where we risk life. If we are not prepared to risk American lives, then the interest is not vital. Most important, if the interest is vital enough to risk lives, then the fact that the Israelis are themselves willing to pay and fight is totally irrelevant to McGovern's argument. Of course, in politics what do you want, good politics or good reasoning?

The end justifies the means:

Charles Lamb's famous tale about the discovery of roast pork is an excellent example of this kind of reasoning. A house where pigs were kept as pets once burned down. While searching in the burnt-out ruins, someone touched one of the dead but now roasted pigs and burned his fingers. Instinctively he put his hand into his mouth to soothe the pain and was thereby the first man to taste roast pork. The new taste sensation was very agreeable. Thereafter, whenever anyone wanted roast pork, he built a house, enclosed some pigs in it, and then proceeded to burn it down. Now if roast pork is a good thing as an end, and if the end justifies the means, then there is nothing inherently absurd about the means used to obtain it. However, when we compare the means used with other possible means, we see quite clearly that the end does not justify the means, precisely because there are far less costly ways of preparing roast pork.

There is another sense in which we talk about the relationship between means and ends. What does one do in a situation in which there is apparently a means to an end but that means conflicts with other ends? We could, for example, remove the problem of the urban poor by exterminating them.

Old and new:

If one is relatively conservative, then he is in favor of preserving the tried and true (old) and opposed to disrespectful young scoundrels engaging in mindless experiments (new). If one is relatively progressive, then he is in favor of novel and bold foresight (new) and opposed to social stagnation (old).

Fire and smoke:

Where there is smoke, there you will find fire. Behind this piece of political wisdom is the view that if there is a great deal of debate, dissension, and discussion then there are serious underlying difficulties which will cause a group to break apart. If there's no smoke then there's no fire. Behind this corollary is the assumption that if there is no vociferous opposition and political activity then the society involved is very stable and all of the members are happy with their lot.

Your neighbor's grass:

Viewing your neighbor's grass can be a very educational experience politically. If you are allergic to grass, imagine you are looking at a neighboring country's social conditions. Depending upon your mood, your neighbor's grass is either greener than yours, in which case there must be something wrong with your gardener (government) or his grass is browner, in which case your gardener must be okay. There are other possibilities which are never recognized. Maybe he has a lousy gardener working with natural resources which are so great that anybody can make the green grass there greener. Maybe you have a marvelous gardener making the best of a bad situation. Unless the comparisons are carefully presented, they will be invidious.

Political thinkers are so ingenious and imaginative that it is impossible to anticipate every kind of move they might make. Nevertheless, the reader should have a good idea from these few instances of what to expect.

CHAPTER FIVE

Cause-and-Effect Reasoning

Although causal reasoning may appear in any part of an argument, either the presentation, attack, or defense, there is a reason why I have devoted a separate chapter to it. Causal reasoning involves some technical points which cannot be treated briefly or separated without confusion and unnecessary repetition. Hence it is important to bring this material together in one place.

CAUSAL REASONING AS PRACTICAL

In daily life we are interested in causes and effects in so far as they affect our lives. If we know the causes of things then we are in a better position to control what happens to us. This is behind the famous remark of Francis Bacon that "knowledge is power." The fact that cause and effect are practical concepts, concepts we employ in the practice of daily life, explains why the common man thinks more of technology than of science. Science is interested in concomitant variation, the relationships among "things" which can be described mathematically. Science is not interested in causation. Technology is the employment of scientific information to control the environment. Technology is very much an affair of cause and effect precisely because it introduces human purposes into the world of concomitant variation.

In practical life we are interested in events from two points of view: how to make things happen, i.e., how to bring them about, and how to prevent things from happening. For instance, as a farmer I want to know how to cause rain when my crops need it. That is, I would like to be able to "cause" rain for the convenience of my crops. At the same time, I would like to know how to prevent it from raining if possible at some times so as to prevent my crops from being ruined. That is, I want to know how to cause it not to rain.

In medicine we want to cure people, that is, to cause them to regain their health. We also want to prevent them from getting ill. Here we want to find the "causes" of disease and eliminate them. In political, social, and economic life we want to know the causes of human happiness so that we can nourish them and the causes of human suffering so that we can eliminate them. To these two ends, bringing about and prevention, there correspond two technical concepts: sufficient and necessary conditions. In this context they will be defined as follows.

A *necessary condition* is a condition (state of affairs, thing, process, etc.) which must be present if we are to obtain the effect. One of the necessary conditions of life as we know it is oxygen. Some of the necessary conditions of a fire are oxygen, a flammable material, etc. If we know the necessary conditions of an event then we can *prevent* it from happening. Remove any one necessary condition and the effect does not take place. Thus we can speak of a necessary condition as a cause or one of the causes of an event.

A *sufficient condition* is a condition (state of affairs, thing, process, etc.) which automatically leads to the production of another event, etc. Swallowing cyanide is a sufficient condition for death. The difference between a necessary and a sufficient condition is that although a necessary condition must be present, by itself it will not produce the effect. The sufficient condition is "sufficient" by itself to produce the effect. Usually the sufficient condition is really a set of necessary conditions, all of which must be present at the same time and place. For instance, a combustible material, oxygen, and the combustion point are all necessary conditions for fire. Together all three constitute the sufficient conditions for a fire. If we know the sufficient condition of an event then we can *produce* it at will. Thus we can speak of a sufficient condition as a cause of an event.

There are then at least two senses in which we talk about causes: causes as necessary conditions and causes as sufficient conditions. In addition, if we consider "cause" in the practical sense we can talk about *multiple causes*. Not only is swallowing cyanide a cause of death, but we can also die by getting a bullet in the heart. There is then a sense in which there can be more than one cause (of the sufficient variety) for an effect. When we talk about necessary conditions it is rather obvious that there can be more than one cause. Suppose one man shoots another. Suppose we want to know what would have prevented that effect. What is the cause? Without bullets there would have been no shooting; the same is true of a firing pin; the same is true of the gun, and so on back into the early childhood, no doubt, of the man who pulled the trigger. All of these are necessary conditions and therefore all of these events or things are causes.

There are several other ways in which causes and effects may be related. There is such a thing as a *causal chain*. For example, if A is the cause of B (where A may be a cause in either the necessary or sufficient condition sense) and B is the cause of C (where B may be a cause in either the necessary or sufficient condition sense), then in a very important sense we may also speak of A being a cause of C. For instance, if the presence of old newspapers in the basement of my house (newspapers are a combustible material and therefore a necessary condition of a fire) is a cause of my house catching fire, and if you are burned as an effect of that fire (fire is a sufficient condition of your being burned), then through the causal chain the newspapers are a cause of your being burned. Historians can make interesting use of causal chains as when they say that had Cleopatra's nose been a half-inch longer the course of world history would have been different.

We also speak of a mutual interaction of causes and effects, but this must be qualified. Let us assume that poverty is a cause (necessary condition) of ignorance in the sense that many poor people are unable to get a good education. Without good education (necessary condition) those same people will be unable to earn enough money to climb out of their poverty. However, poverty was present before the lack of education. Nevertheless, the lack of education is a cause for not overcoming that poverty. Here one thing is the cause of another thing or effect and that effect becomes a cause for another effect (causal chain) which is *like* the original cause. It is important to note this qualification because in our example someone might say that poverty is a cause of ignorance (this is true enough) and that ignorance is a cause of poverty (which may be misleading). It would be more accurate in this case to say that ignorance is a "cause" of not overcoming that poverty.

HUME'S DEFINITION OF CAUSE AND EFFECT

The clearest definition of the relationship between cause and effect (the reader is reminded that this is philosophically controversial) was provided by the great British philosopher David Hume (1711–76). According to Hume we are justified in saying that one thing is the cause (C) and another thing is the effect (E) if the following three conditions hold:

(1) C, the cause, *preceded* E, the effect, in time;
(2) C and E are *contiguous* in time and place; and
(3) there is a *history* of regularity in the precedence and contiguity of C and E.

Hume's analysis, of course, has to be qualified. He does this but I shall select only the part of it that concerns us here. We always talk about the cause preceding the effect for practical reasons. We want to be able to control events in advance so we look for conditions which take place prior in time to the event we want to control. Technically speaking, some causes are simultaneous with their effects, as when we say that the striking of the match is the cause of the match's lighting. It would be hair splitting to insist that the striking preceded the lighting in that there is clearly a sense in which both happen at the same time. Therefore we might be a little more accurate and say that the cause must precede, or be simultaneous with, the effect, or perhaps that no cause can follow the effect.

Second, there must be some more or less clear connection in time and space between the two events that we are connecting causally. We say that a specific fire is the cause of a specific effect, smoke, and we can see the smoke coming from that specific fire (space and time). When we say that a germ caused Mr. Smith to become ill, the germ and the illness both take place in Mr. Smith's body. Even when two distant events are causally related we speak of the intervening series of causes and effects forming a chain between the two events. For instance, the assassination of Archduke Franz Ferdinand at Sarajevo is a "cause" (allegedly) of World War I because of a whole series of intervening diplomatic and military events. Even where we do not know for sure the exact connection, we always suspect some kind of spatio-temporal link which we expect to discover later. No doubt the concept of contiguity would have to be redefined in terms of contemporary physics, but the everyday sense of it is well understood.

Third, and most important, is the history of regularity. Hume distinguishes between a natural psychological tendency (which depends on a single instance of succession) to suspect a causal relation and the logical justification in believing there to be a causal connection (which depends upon a long history of regularity). For example, if while having dinner I drink some wine and the lights suddenly go out I may be psychologically tempted to think that my drinking wine causes lights to go out. However, there is no past experience to justify this belief. The connection between turning the light switch and the light's going out has had such a long history of regularity that it would be irrational not to believe in their causal connection. It is the history of regularity which is usually crucial in settling conflicts over what caused what. This is why past experience is so important in documenting a case or position you want to defend.

MILL'S METHODS

John Stuart Mill was a noted British philosopher and logician of the nineteenth century. In his famous work *System of Logic* (1843) he developed what he called "methods" for the analysis of causes and effects in specific situations. What follows is our translation of those methods into our previous scheme for discussing cause and effect.

Suppose you were interested in finding out which circumstances preceding (cause) an event or phenomenon or which circumstances following (effect) that event or phenomenon were really connected causally with that event or phenomenon. Mill suggests that we do this by comparing different instances of the event or phenomenon and then try to discover in what respects they agree and in what respects they differ.

Method of Agreement.

"If two or more instances of the phenomenon under investigation have only one circumstance in common, the circumstance in which alone all of the instances agree is the cause (or effect) of the given phenomenon."

Suppose you are giving a party at which various

foods and beverages are served. After a while a number of people at the party begin to act strangely, that is, they talk very loudly, laugh at anything, begin to undress, and play various assorted pranks. In short, they are drunk. What caused these people at your party to get drunk? Was it the food? No, because everybody tasted the food and many did not get drunk. Was it the beverages? You examine the beverages and find that all of them are alcoholic (all beverages agree in having one circumstance in common) and all of the people who are inebriated drank the alcoholic beverages. Therefore, you may conclude that alcoholic beverages caused people at your party to become drunk.

The method of agreement is effective because of certain assumptions and background information operative in any analysis. Mill has emphasized in his definition of the method that there is only one circumstance in common. For example, suppose the people who were drunk had had gin and soda, Scotch and soda, rum and soda, etc. Then soda would be a circumstance in common. It is because we already know that soda does not cause drunkenness or because we may have eliminated it on the grounds that someone drank straight soda and did not get drunk that we are finally led to alcohol.

What the method of agreement does most effectively is to eliminate from consideration certain factors as not being necessary conditions for the production of an effect. For example, someone might think that standing under the mistletoe at the party is a cause of drunkenness. However, by finding a case of a person who is drunk but who did not stand under the mistletoe we have a case of the phenomenon without the suspected condition being present. Since the effect can occur without that condition, then that condition (standing under the mistletoe) cannot be a necessary condition of being drunk.

Method of Difference.

"If an instance in which the phenomenon under investigation occurs and an instance in which it does not occur have every circumstance in common save one, that one occurring only in the former, the circumstance in which alone the two instances differ is the effect, or the cause, or an indispensable part of the cause of the phenomenon."

Suppose a set of male twins boards a plane and sits together. Later during the plane trip one of them becomes violently ill. What is the cause? The answer is found by locating one condition which is different when there are no other differing conditions. Both have the same general health, performed the same activities before boarding the plane, sat in the same area (they even periodically exchanged seats), etc. The stewardess, however, remembers that everyone on the plane including one of the twin brothers had steak for lunch, whereas the other twin was the only person who had something else for lunch (lobster). Since this is the only circumstance in which they differ then the lobster lunch must be the cause of the man's illness.

What the method of difference does most effectively is to eliminate from consideration certain factors as not being sufficient conditions for the production of an effect. For example, someone might have argued that the before-lunch cocktail on the plane might have been the cause of the illness. However, since both men had a cocktail and one of them did not get sick, then having the cocktail does not lead by itself automatically to getting sick. Hence the cocktail is not a sufficient condition for causing the illness on the plane.

Joint Method of Agreement and Difference. "If two or more instances in which the phenomenon occurs have only one circumstance in common, while two or more instances in which it does not occur have nothing in common save the absence of that circumstance, the circumstance in which alone the two sets of instances differ is the effect, or the cause, or an indispensable part of the cause, of the phenomenon."

Suppose you were at a party where five kinds of punch were prepared and each punch had its ingredients marked on its respective bowl. All together there were five ingredients:

> A. cranberry juice
> B. orange slices
> C. sugar
> D. seltzer
> E. rye whisky

The five punches had different combinations and only some of the punches tasted good. What was the "cause" of the good taste? Let us schematize the available combinations and assume that no further experimentation is possible.

> Punch 1 ingredients: ABC E (good taste)
> Punch 2 ingredients: A   DE (good taste)
> Punch 3 ingredients: B   DE (good taste)
> Punch 4 ingredients: A C   (bad taste)
> Punch 5 ingredients: B D   (bad taste)

To review, Punch 5 had only orange slices and seltzer in it. Looking at the first two punches we could not use the method of agreement. However, when we take into account Punch 3 we can see by the method of agreement that E, rye whisky, might be the cause of good taste. Can we use the method of difference to check out if the absence of rye whisky will lead to bad taste? Only if we can make two punches with everything in common except E can we use the method of difference. However we cannot use it here, because while Punches 4 and 5 lack E they are different in too many other respects. However, the joint method does tell us that E is the cause (necessarily) of the good taste. Thus the joint method works when the method of difference cannot be used. The joint method eliminates D, B, C, and A as necessary conditions of good tasting punch, and it eliminates A, C, B, and D as sufficient conditions of good tasting punch.

One might conclude from this that the main ingredient of a good party is a knowledge of Mill's methods.

FALLACIES OF CAUSAL REASONING

As a result of the two previous sections, all of the following fallacies concerning causal reasoning will appear to be due either to a violation of Hume's three criteria of cause and effect or to a violation of Mill's methods concerning the elimination of necessary and sufficient conditions.

Concomitant Variation.

This is the fallacy of assuming that because two events show a high incidence of correlation they are therefore causally connected. This is especially true of statistical correlations. For example, the rapid increase of college enrollments during the decade of the 1920s varies concomitantly with rapid increase in the number of inmates in institutions for the mentally ill. Is there a causal connection? Hardly. This variation satisfies none of Hume's criteria: there is no indication of which event preceded which, there is no connection seen or imaginable between these events spatially, and no history of regularity prior to the decade of the 1920s.

Statistical correlation between lung cancer and cigarette smoking is acceptable as an instance of causal reasoning because it does satisfy the criteria: cigarette smoking precedes lung cancer, independent research on the effects of nicotine on the skin of mice makes a spatial connection imaginable, and there is now a long history of such correlation.

What about the relationship between night and day? Doesn't day follow night and night day with unerring regularity? Does this mean that night causes day or does day cause night? The answer is obvious: while night and day do satisfy the two criteria of a history of regularity and spatial connection, they do not satisfy the criterion of temporal priority because we cannot tell whether night precedes day or whether day regularly precedes night. Since no one can say, then we do not have the right to say that either one does and therefore the example does not fit the three criteria.

There is another famous example called the example of the occasionalist clocks. Imagine two clocks, A and B, where allegedly clock A is five minutes ahead of Clock B. Every hour on the hour the clocks chime. Since A regularly chimes before B, does this imply that A is the cause of B?

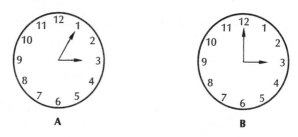

A   B

The diagram is useful because it shows that it is impossible to state any general relation of temporal priority between the two clocks. Clock A may be viewed as five minutes ahead of Clock B, but Clock B may also be viewed as eleven hours and fifty-five minutes ahead of Clock A. Consequently, the example of the two clocks does not meet the requirement of temporal priority. In addition, there is no spatial connection between the two clocks.

Known Counterexample.

The following fallacy is committed, so far as I know, only by philosophers and logicians. Imagine that at twelve o'clock a siren goes off at a factory signaling the lunch hour. At the same time a train leaves the railroad station every day at the noon hour. Does the siren cause the train to leave? The example would seem to fit the criteria of temporal precedence and historical regularity. However, to begin with there is no clear spatial connection. More important, the example really does not fit the criterion of historical regularity since all of us already know from past experience (a) that the siren does not cause the train to depart and (b) that if the siren did not go off the train would depart anyway; that is, we know the real cause of the train's departure.

It should be noted that the examples of night and day and the occasionalist clocks are also examples of the fallacy of known counterexample.

Post Hoc.

The original Latin expression is *"post hoc, ergo propter hoc"* which when translated means "after this, therefore because of this." It is a fallacy of causal reasoning in that it is based on the mistaken belief that mere temporal priority constitutes a causal relation. It completely neglects the other criteria of spatial connection and a history of regularity.

There are some amusing and some not so amusing examples of the *post hoc* fallacy. For example, Mrs. Smith prays that her husband will recover from the mumps and he does. She assumes that since the prayer preceded the recovery then the prayer must be the cause of the recovery.

In advertising, this sort of fallacy appears quite frequently. There are endless testimonials about how people recovered after taking Dr. Hippocrates' snake oil. Without some other evidence of a connection and some historical laboratory evidence there is no good reason to believe that the snake oil really was the cause of the recovery. We all know that cold remedies cure a cold in seven days and that without the remedy the cold takes a week to go away.

In political discussions I have heard the following examples of the *post hoc* fallacy. It has been argued that one of the consequences of the atom bombing of Hiroshima was the cold war. There is temporal precedence here but surely no spatial connection and no historical basis for this assertion. If anything, history shows that the cold war would have come about anyway if it were not already in existence. More recently, I have heard that Vice President Agnew's speeches (or Spock's book on raising children) were the cause of the deaths at Kent State in May 1970. So far this suggestion has nothing to recommend it except the *post hoc* connection.

Irreversible Order.

Here we shall begin discussing examples of fallacies in causal reasoning which violate some of Mill's methods by confusing and misusing distinctions between necessary and sufficient conditions. The fallacy of irreversible order is based on the assumption that if A causes B, then B cannot be the cause of A. For example, the existence of poverty in some countries prevents them from sponsoring universities and even simple programs to raise the literacy rate. Thus clearly *poverty is a cause of ignorance*. At the same time, there are historical examples of how the closing of the universities (e.g., Spain and Italy during the Inquisition) led eventually to impoverishing the economy as a whole. Thus, clearly, *ignorance can cause poverty*. In terms of the distinction between necessary and sufficient conditions, the fallacy of irreversible order incorrectly assumes that if A is a sufficient condition of B, then B cannot be a sufficient condition for A.

Denying the Antecedent.

The best way to see this fallacy is to show first a correct argument and then an incorrect one using the fallacy.

> *If* you take cyanide *then* you will die.
> *You take cyanide.*
> *Therefore,* you will die.

Schematically the argument looks like this:

> *If . . . S₁ . . . then . . . S₂*
> S₁.
> *Therefore, S₂.*

Now let us look at an incorrect form of the argument.

> If you take cyanide then you will die.
> You do *not*-take cyanide.
> Therefore, you will *not*-die.

Schematically the argument looks like this.

> If . . . S₁ . . . then . . . S₂.
> Not-S₁.
> Therefore, not-S₂.

You can now see the difference between the two arguments. A sentence of the form if . . . then is called a conditional sentence. The part of the conditional sentence following the "if" is called the antecedent. In the second example above, the antecedent is denied and that is why it is called denying the antecedent. Now it should be intuitively obvious that the second example is an example of poor or fallacious reasoning, whereas the first example is a true example of causal reasoning. Why? The answer is simple. The second example is wrong because there are other causes of death besides swallowing cyanide. Even if I do not take cyanide I will eventually die some other way. In terms of necessary conditions, the *fallacy of denying the antecedent is the fallacy of believing that S₁ (cyanide) is a necessary condition* of death *when* in actuality *it is a sufficient condition.*

Affirming the Consequent.

This fallacy is very similar to the one we discussed above. We are still dealing with conditional sentences (if . . . then) and the part of the conditional sentence following the "then" is called the consequent. We can use the same example.

> *If* I take cyanide *then* I die.
> I die.
> *Therefore* I took cyanide.

Schematically the argument looks like this:

> *If* . . . S_1 . . . *then* . . . S_2.
> S_2.
> *Therefore,* S_1.

The correct scheme, you will recall, is:

> *If* . . . S_1 . . . *then* . . . S_2.
> S_1.
> *Therefore,* S_2.

The difference between the two schemes is obvious. In the fallacious one we have reversed the order of S_1 and S_2. We have *affirmed the consequent,* hence the name of the fallacy, when we should have affirmed the antecedent. The fact that I died does not automatically imply that I took cyanide even if the first sentence about cyanide causing death is true. Obviously there are other causes of death besides cyanide. Actually, in terms of necessary and sufficient conditions the error here is the same as the error of denying the antecedent; it is the *fallacy of assuming that a sufficient condition is a necessary one.* Cyanide is a sufficient condition of dying but not a necessary one.

Genetic Fallacy.

We have already seen several examples of genetic arguments, an argument or explanation of how a belief came about or how someone comes to believe something. Such explanations, when true, are perfectly legitimate, useful, and enlightening. There is, however, a special form of this argument which is quite fallacious.

Suppose I argue that the presence of oxygen in a forest preserve was *the* cause of a forest fire. Now it is true that if there had been no oxygen in the forest there certainly would have been no forest fire. It is also true that if there had been no lightning or a dropped match, etc., there would have been no forest fire. In other words, when it is assumed that one of several necessary conditions was the sole and exclusive cause of an effect we have a genetic fallacy.

Another example concerns the deaths of several students on the campus of Kent State University in May 1970. The students were shot by National Guardsmen. It may be argued that if the National Guard had had better training they would not have shot the students. It may also be argued that if the college had not called the Guard in the first place surely (as a necessary condition) no students would have been shot. If, however, one insists that this was the *sole* way of preventing the deaths then he is guilty of the genetic fallacy. Surely if there had been no student demonstrations (necessary condition of calling the Guard) there would have been no deaths. Which necessary condition one chooses to emphasize is a matter, too often, of political expediency.

The same kind of fallacy is found when one excuses a criminal for his crime on the grounds that (genetically and necessarily) he committed his crime as a result of environmental factors. In reply we may note that the legal system (genetically and necessarily) must find the defendant guilty and punish him. We would have to "understand" the judge, jury, prosecutor, and executioner because they too are victims of their environment. Perhaps a more interesting question is not what caused the crime, but what would be the effects of punishing or not punishing the defendant.

CHAPTER SIX

Formal Analysis
of Arguments

The purpose of this chapter is twofold: to summarize that part of traditional Aristotelian logic which is useful in analyzing arguments, and to indicate how informal logic may be viewed as highly developed subdivision of traditional logic.

IDENTIFYING ARGUMENTS

In offering an argument one tries to convince or persuade others of a position or belief. The belief one wants others to accept is the *conclusion* of the argument. By definition, each argument has one and only one conclusion. The reasons or evidence which one offers for the conclusion are called *premises*. An argument may have any number of premises. In addition, in order to prove one's conclusion one may offer a series of interlocking arguments in which some conclusions are premises to other arguments so that the final conclusion follows from the whole series.

Before you can construct or reconstruct an argument you must know how to identify a premise and how to identify a conclusion. Customarily, certain key words are used to signal to the audience that a statement is either a premise or a conclusion.

The key words most often used as identification marks for premises are *since, for,* and *because*. Usually any sentence following these words is a premise.

The key words most often used as identification marks for conclusions are *therefore, thus, hence,* and *consequently*. Usually any sentence following these words is a conclusion.

Consider the following example: "Since all men are mortal, and since Socrates is a man, we may therefore conclude that Socrates is mortal." Using our key words we may reconstruct the argument as follows:

Premise: All men are mortal.

Premise: Socrates is a man.

Conclusion: Socrates is mortal.

Most people are usually sensitive enough to the rules of language so that it is often not necessary to use so many keys. Hence there is a tendency to use the minimum number of such key words and occasionally we even leave out a premise if we think that it is implicitly understood. For example: "Jones cannot vote because he is not registered." Here we have only one key word, "because." We now know that what follows "because" is a premise.

Premise: He (Jones) is not registered (to vote).

If what follows "because" is a premise then what precedes it (and all premise key words) must be the conclusion.

Conclusion: Jones cannot vote.

The premise is quite obviously the reason or evidence for the conclusion. It is also apparent that there is some additional information which the author of the statement believes that his audience already knows so that there is no need to spell it out. That additional information is called the "suppressed" premise:

Suppressed premise: Only those who are registered can vote.

Now let us look at the reconstructed argument as a whole:

Premise: Only those who are registered can vote.

Premise: Jones is not registered.

Conclusion: Jones cannot vote.

As a final example I offer an interlocking argument. "We ought not to vote for Jones because he is dishonest, and we have all known that since the scandal broke." According to our key words, we may note the following:

Premise: He (Jones) is dishonest.

Premise: A scandal broke (involving Jones).

Conclusion: We ought not to vote for Jones.

While the argument is convincing, it is not clear from its present form how the evidence is related to the conclusion. Let us add a few suppressed but obvious premises:

Suppressed premise: Wherever we find political scandals we find dishonesty.

Suppressed premise: We ought not to vote for dishonest people.

We now have, apparently, four premises and one conclusion. However, if you go back to the original argument you will see that a sentence preceded "since" and must be a conclusion. That sentence is "He (Jones) is dishonest." But this sentence is also a premise because it is preceded by the word "because." Here we have a perfect example of a sentence that is the premise to one argument and the conclusion of another. The two conclusions signal us that we have two interlocking arguments. We reconstruct them as follows:

Argument I

Premise: Wherever we find political scandals we find dishonesty.

Premise: Jones was convicted of being involved in a scandal.

Conclusion: Jones is dishonest.

Argument II

Premise: We ought not to vote for dishonest people.

Premise: Jones is dishonest.

Conclusion: We ought not to vote for Jones.

Notice that the conclusion to the first argument is the second premise in the second argument.

SYLLOGISMS

In this chapter and throughout the book we have been implicitly following the practice of using, for the most part, arguments which have consisted of two premises. Such arguments having two premises are known as syllogisms. The reason they are used so often is more than a matter of convenience and tradition. All arguments can be reconstructed as syllogisms, that is, as having two premises and a conclusion. In addition, such reconstructed arguments are easier to follow. Most important, as we shall see below, informal logic can be usefully viewed as an exercise in syllogistic reasoning involving some very questionable suppressed premises.

Although there are several different kinds of syllogisms, we shall be concerned here with categorical syllogisms. A categorical syllogism is a syllogism where all of the statements, both premises and the conclusion, are categorical statements. A statement is categorical if it is of the subject predicate form. That is, it is a statement with four distinguishable parts: a quantifier, a subject, a copula, and a predicate. The following four statements are categorical:

quantifier	subject	copula	predicate	code
1. All	crows	are	black.	A
2. No	crows	are	black.	E
3. Some	crows	are	black.	I
4. Some	crows	are-not	black.	O

I have used the same subject matter for the sake of convenience. We are not concerned here with the truth or falsity of these statements but only their form.

Categorical statements may also be classified as either affirmative or negative. Statements one and three above are *affirmative* in that they affirm something (namely the predicate) of the subject. Statements two and four are *negative* in that they deny something of the subject (namely the predicate). When we talk about the statements being affirmative or negative we are speaking of the *quality* of the statement.

In addition to a quality, statements have quantity. The quantity of a statement refers to the relationship between the quantifier and the subject term. There are three kinds of quantity: universal, particular, and singular. A statement is *universal* when the subject term refers to the entire class of objects which it names. Thus statements one and two above are universal in that they both refer to the entire class of crows. A statement is *particular* when the subject term does not refer to the entire class of objects it names; rather it refers only to *some* part of that class. Thus statements three and four above are particular in that they both refer to some part of the class of crows.

A statement is *singular* when the subject term is a proper name referring to a single individual. Our chart above does not include any examples of singular statements. An example would be the following: "Aristotle was a great logician." Another example is "Bob Dylan is not a logician." By convention, all singular statements are treated as universal statements on the grounds that they refer to the whole of the subject (all of Aristotle, all of Bob Dylan). In addition, the example about Aristotle is affirmative and the example about Bob Dylan is negative. Using the code from the chart above, the statement about Aristotle is an A statement, like "All crows are black," and the statement about Bob Dylan is an E statement, like "No crows are black."

Again using the code letters A, E, I, and O, we summarize our discussion so far in the following:

A: Universal affirmative   I: Particular affirmative

E: Universal negative   O: Particular negative

The concept of quantity refers primarily to the relationship of subject term and quantifier. Quantity overlaps with another concept, distribution, which refers to the predicate term as well as to the subject term. A term (either subject or predicate) is *distributed* if it refers to the whole class it names. A term is *undistributed* if it refers not to the whole class it names, but to only part of the class. As is obvious from our discussion of quantity, the subject of an A statement (all crows) and the subject of an E statement (no crows) are both distributed. Moreover, the subject of an I statement (some crows) and an O statement (some crows) are both undistributed. Now let us examine the predicates.

The predicate of an A statement ("All crows are black") is undistributed since we are not referring to all black things. The predicate of an E statement ("No crows are black") is distributed since we are saying that nowhere in the entire class of black things will we find a crow. The predicate of an I statement ("Some crows are black") is undistributed since, again, we are not referring to all black things. The predicate of an O statement ("Some crows are not black") is distributed since we can only say that some crows are excluded from the class of black things if we have excluded them from the entire class of black things. The discussion of distribution now looks like this:

Statement	Subject	Predicate
A	distributed	undistributed
E	distributed	distributed
I	undistributed	undistributed
O	undistributed	distributed

There is one other set of relationships among statements that should be noted. A *contradiction* exists between two statements if they both cannot be true or both cannot be false at the same time. A and O are contradictories: If "All crows are black" is true then "Some crows are not black" must be false, and vice versa. Two statements are said to be contraries if it is possible for both to be false but not possible for both to be true at the same time. A and E are contraries since it is possible for "All crows are black" and "No crows are black" both to be false if it is the case that only some crows are black. At the same time if "All crows are black" is true then "No crows are black" cannot be true.

Earlier in the book, in Chapter Two, we showed how one could embarrass an opponent by attacking the contrary of an argument rather than its contradictory. Take the following example: You wish to argue the A statement that "All Communists are bad" and your opponent wishes to argue that "Some Communists are not bad," which is an O statement. In attacking him you pretend that his position is an E and not an O and attack with ease the E proposition "No Communists are bad." While both of you cannot be right—that is, one of you must be wrong either way—the attack on E allows for both of you to be wrong. This is a safety valve in case you find yourself trapped.

The traditional square of opposition brings out the foregoing relationships.

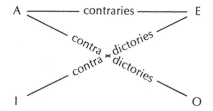

Now that we have examined and defined the properties of categorical statements, it is time to turn our attention to categorical syllogisms. Each statement has two terms, a subject term and a predicate term. Since a syllogism has two premises and a conclusion, a total of three statements, there is a grand total of six terms. However, in a syllogism each of those terms appears twice. Thus a categorical syllogism has three terms each of which appears twice. Example:

All carp are fish.

All fish are found in water.

Therefore, all carp are found in water.

As you can see, "fish" appears twice, "carp" appears twice, and "found in water" appears twice.

We may next distinguish among the major, minor, and middle terms. The *major term* is that term which appears as the predicate of the conclusion. In our example above "found in water" is the major term. The premise which also contains the other appearance of the major term is called the major premise, and in our example "All fish are found in water" is the major premise. The *minor term* is that term which appears as the subject of the conclusion. In our example above "carp" is the minor term. The premise which also contains the other appearance of the minor term is called the minor premise, and in our example "All carp are fish" is the minor premise. Thus every categorical syllogism consists of a major premise, a minor premise, and a conclusion. The *middle term* is the term which appears in both premises. In our example above, "fish" is the middle term.

RULES FOR VALID SYLLOGISMS

We are now ready to test syllogisms. We distinguish between valid and invalid syllogisms. In a *valid* categorical syllogism, if both premises are true then the conclusion must be true. Logicians have been able to work out a few rules such that any syllogism that violates these rules is invalid, and any syllogism that does not violate the rules is automatically valid. Thus we might speak of the rules for invalidating the syllogism.

First, an example of a valid syllogism which is in essence the basic format of all valid syllogistic arguments:

All carp are fish.
All fish are animals.
All carp are animals.

Another version of this same essential form is:

All men are mortal.
Socrates is a man.
Socrates is mortal.

A final version:

All children like candy.
Some members of my household are children.
Some members of my household like candy.

There are three rules, the violation of any of which automatically shows the categorical syllogism to be invalid.

First Rule: The middle term must be distributed at least once. This rule is the only rule that is seriously and frequently violated in everyday reasoning. For example:

All Communists are in favor of reform.
All liberals are in favor of reform.
All liberals are Communists.

In the above argument, the middle term is "in favor of reform." Both premises, in which the middle term occurs, are A statements and the middle term is the predicate in both premises. We know from our chart above on distribution that the predicate of an A statement is never distributed. Therefore the middle term is not distributed at least once and the argument is invalid. The fallacy of *guilt by association* is a form of this kind of invalidity.

Second Rule: A term which is distributed in the conclusion must be distributed in one of the premises.

For example:
> All Communists are in favor of reform.
> No conservatives are Communists.
> No conservatives are in favor of reform.

In the above argument, we have an E statement for the conclusion "No conservatives are in favor of reform." Thus both the subject and the predicate are distributed. However, in the major premise "All Communists are in favor of reform," which is an A statement, the predicate "in favor of reform" cannot be distributed. Thus there is a term "in favor of reform" which is distributed in the conclusion but not in one of the premises and the argument is invalid.

Knowing this rule is especially important when your opponent employs an argument with a suppressed premise. Suppose your opponent uses the following argument: "Since no conservatives are Communists they cannot be in favor of reform." Your reply is twofold. First, you reconstruct your opponent's argument in order to make it valid; supply the missing premise that would make it valid ("All those in favor of reform are Communists"), and ask him if this is what he means. If he says yes, then obviously he is making a false statement and he is embarrassed in front of the audience. Presumably everyone knows that Communists are not the only people in favor of reform. Second, you reconstruct your opponent's argument to make it invalid and supply the missing premise that would make it invalid ("All Communists are in favor of reform") and then expose the argument as invalid and your opponent as a logical ignoramus.

Third Rule: The number of negative premises must be the same as the number of negative conclusions. This rule sounds odd but just think of the possibilities.

Since there is one conclusion, (a) if the conclusion is negative then there must be one, and only one, negative premise. As soon as there are two negative premises the argument is automatically invalid. (b) If the conclusion is affirmative there can be no negative premises. If there is a negative premise there must be a negative conclusion.

The importance of this rule is that it shows one cannot reach a positive conclusion from negative premises. To show that a thing lacks one quality does not prove that it has another. To reach a positive or affirmative conclusion you must have affirmative premises.

For example: Suppose your opponent argues that "Country X is not a capitalist country, therefore Country X respects the working man." There is no possible way of making this a valid argument.

All (or No) Countries which respect the working man are capitalist countries.

Country X is not a capitalist country.

∴ Country X is a country that respects the working man.

Either way the above argument is invalid. The only way to get to the affirmative conclusion desired is to present the affirmative argument:

All noncapitalist countries are countries which respect the working man.

Country X is a noncapitalist country.

∴ Country X is a country that respects the working man.

However, by making the argument valid we expose its Achilles heel or most questionable point. Why should we accept the statement that "All noncapitalist countries are countries which respect the working man"? Not only is this sentence not intuitively obvious, it is downright false. Once again, knowing the rules helps us to expose the implicit generalizations of your opponent's case.

We have defined a valid argument as an argument that does not violate the rules so that *if* its premises are true *then* its conclusion must be true. However this does not mean that a valid argument automatically has true premises. *Arguments can be valid and still have false premises.*

However, when an argument is valid (i.e., it does not violate the rules) and its premises are known to be true, then we say it is a *sound* argument.

It is my contention that one rarely finds invalid arguments in daily life. On the other hand, one finds an incredible number of unsound arguments. This is precisely why knowing about the syllogism is useful. By reconstructing your opponent's arguments to make them valid, and thereby bringing out the implicit premise (usually the major premise), you can put your finger on some generalization which might be weak enough to be attacked. We have seen this in the second and third rules above. When you attack that premise as untrue you are accusing your opponent of having an unsound argument.

Further, most, if not all, of the traditional *fallacies of informal logic may be viewed as valid* arguments *but* with an unacceptable major premise, and therefore as *unsound arguments.* For example, the fallacy of composition is the fallacy of believing that what is true of all the parts is true of the whole:

All that is true of the parts *is* true of the whole.

All of the parts of a locomotive are light.

Therefore, a (whole) locomotive is light.

Since the argument is valid but the conclusion false (or unacceptable), one of the premises must be false (or unacceptable).

The fallacious use of the *ad populum* is an appeal to the major premise that what most people like is good. Consider the following argument:

Whatever book most people like is great literature.

Most people like *Love Story*.

Therefore, *Love Story* is great literature.

The second premise is true if one judges by best seller lists. The conclusion is considered false by many literary experts. At the same time, the argument is logically valid. The only way of challenging the conclusion is to argue that the major premise ("Whatever book most people like is great literature") is false, and therefore that the argument is unsound.

The *ad baculum* or the appeal to force can also be viewed as an instance of an unsound argument. Consider the following argument:

Whenever I threaten you is a time when you must do as I say.

Now is a time I threaten to raise your taxes if you do not vote for Smith.

Now is a time that you must do as I say (vote for Smith).

The argument is valid but unsound if you reject as false the premise that you must do as I say whenever I threaten you.

I shall leave to the reader the task of working out examples of other well-known fallacies. Knowing syllogistic logic thus helps to analyze the weak points in your opponent's arguments.

Appendix

The following appendix is intended as a tool, a reading guide, for helping the reader to ask the right kind of questions when he reads a work which is designed to present an argument. Not only will these questions, when raised in appropriate circumstances, improve reading comprehension, but they should also help to develop more analytical and critical perspective on argumentative works.

I.   What is the *problem?*
    A. How is the problem formulated?
    B. Why is this problem an important one?
    C. What is the history of this problem?
    D. Which prominent personalities have been interested in this problem?

II. What *solutions* to the problem are there?
    A. What are the conclusions reached?
    B. By what argument(s) is the conclusion reached?
    C. What facts or assumptions serve as premises?
    D. When a prominent personality offers a solution, does he also argue for or against other prominent personalities?
        Does he raise objections to alternative solutions?
        Does he consider objections to his own solutions?

III. *Evaluation*
    A. What are the advantages and disadvantages of the alternative formulations to the problem?

B.   Has the importance or history of the problem ever
     been misrepresented?
C.   Are the solutions logically related to the premises?
D.   Are the facts true? Are the assumptions accept-
     able? Are the objections answerable?

Index

120-21
49-56